COOKING
WITH
SCRAPS

COOKING WITH SCRAPS

TURN YOUR PEELS, CORES, RINDS, AND STEMS INTO DELICIOUS MEALS

Lindsay-Jean Hard

WORKMAN PUBLISHING · NEW YORK

Library of Congress Cataloging-in-Publication Data is available.

ISBN 978-0-7611-9303-6

Design by Lisa Hollander
Photography by Penny De Los Santos
Food Stylist: Nora Singley
Prop Stylist: Sara Abalan
Additional photos and icons: **Adobe Stock:** pp. ix–xiii (icons), 2, 7, 10, 14, 17, 18, 20, 22, 23, 25, 28, 31, 36 (icon), 38, 42, 46–47, 55, 58, 60, 63, 67, 74, 80, 82, 84 (icon), 86, 89, 93, 96–97, 103, 107–108, 111, 115, 120, 122, 124, 126, 129 (icon), 132, 136, 138, 140–141, 146, 148 (icon), 150–151, 153–155, 158, 163–164, 166, 169–170, 172, 175, 177. **Shutterstock:** p. xix Elena Elisseeva, p. xviii Jack Jelly (left), p. xviii Alen Kadr (right), p. xxi maryloo, p. xvii NinaM, p. 54 SOMMAI, p. xx A. Zhuravleva.

Workman books are available at special discounts when purchased in bulk for premiums and sales promotions as well as for fund-raising or educational use. Special editions or book excerpts can also be created to specification. For details, contact the Special Sales Director at the address below, or send an email to specialmarkets@workman.com.

Workman Publishing Company, Inc.
225 Varick Street
New York, NY 10014-4381
workman.com

WORKMAN is a registered trademark of Workman Publishing Co., Inc.

Printed in China
First printing October 2018

10 9 8 7 6 5 4 3 2 1

To Mike,

my partner in
life and love,
and my
favorite person
to cook for.

Contents

CLEAN *out the* **CRISPER**

QUICK PICKLES
Tangy Fridge Pickles
PAGE 58

Pickled Vegetables

CLEAN *out the* **CRISPER**

SALTS
Tomato Skin Salt
PAGE 82

CLEAN *out the* **CRISPER**

SUGARS
Pear Peel Cinnamon Sugar
PAGE 84

Avocado Pasta with a Crunchy Cilantro Stem Sprinkle

Watermelon Rind–Lime Granita with Basil Whipped Cream

Hello there!

I don't think there are any perfect recipes.

If you find this to be a disconcerting beginning to a cookbook, a book that by name is made up entirely of recipes, bear with me.

There are many, many recipes that are so good, they're incredibly popular or have stood the test of time (or both!): Yotam Ottolenghi and Sami Tamimi's Basic Hummus (from *Jerusalem*), the Plum Torte that Marian Burros made famous (published regularly in the *New York Times*), and Marcella Hazan's Tomato Sauce (from her *Essentials of Classic Italian Cooking*), just to name a few.

When I say that no recipes are "perfect," I mean in the sense that they are not immutable—there's no recipe that is above tweaking. From Ottolenghi and Tamimi, I've learned that cooking the soaked chickpeas for a short period of time with baking soda allows them to puree smoother than I ever thought possible, making this hummus an invaluable addition to my cooking repertoire, and the inspiration for my Kale Stem Hummus (page 109). I find I prefer to use less tahini than called for in the Ottolenghi-Tamimi recipe, which is merely a reflection of my taste rather than a critique of the original recipe. Since 1983, the Plum Torte made famous by Marian Burros has been published on an almost annual basis in the *New York Times*, due in part to reader demand. Not only has the amount of sugar called for decreased over time, but the *Times* also published an article with five ways to adapt the torte. And while I love Marcella Hazan's Tomato Sauce just as it is—it's the inspiration for the sauce in my Collard Stem and Lemony Ricotta Stuffed Shells (page 87)—I've always hated

that the onion is discarded after cooking, so I blend it right in.

All of this is to say that while recipes may well be very good, or even pretty much perfect, just as they are written, that doesn't mean they are beyond messing with, tweaking, and adapting to your preferences. They aren't. And you should. That's why I'll remind you to taste and adjust seasonings at every turn—sometimes we can forget that a touch more salt or an additional squeeze of lemon is all it takes to really make a dish sing. And for most of the recipes within these pages I give you suggestions for just how to play around with them, because while I've written these recipes to be perfect just as they are, that doesn't mean that they will be for you. I sincerely hope you take the ideas within these pages and make them your own.

To that end, because recipes aren't created in a vacuum—we all draw inspiration from those around us—I've tried to note who influenced me in the headnotes of recipes whenever possible. I want to express my gratitude for their formative ideas and recipes and I want to make sure you're introduced to them as well, in case you want to check out more of what they're doing.

Let's back up for a minute to tell you a little bit more about who I am and why I wrote this book.

One of my very favorite picture books from childhood was *The Boy Who Ate Flowers*. If you haven't read this 1960 classic by Nancy Sherman, the title pretty much sums it up. Peter, the boy, begins to tire of eating oatmeal and he goes in search of new culinary experiences . . . in his mother's flower garden. Unfazed that everyone thinks Peter has lost his mind, I delighted in the fact that Peter had found a tasty, underappreciated food source—made even better with the eventual help of a French flower chef.

Fast-forward a couple of decades, and I was putting my master's degree in urban planning to use in a quasi-governmental office job. At the time, Ann Arbor, Michigan, didn't have single-stream recycling (a system in which all recyclables are commingled instead of sorted), and was only processing #1 and #2 plastics—everything else was simply thrown away. I was aghast and created new signs for the recycle bins in our office building, instructing everyone to recycle *all* plastics—#1 through #7. I then regularly collected all of that recycling, along with my personal stash of plastic, and carted it with me across the state every time I visited my parents so that they could add it to their single-stream recycling bin. While they appreciated my tree-hugging

inclinations, they, and their overflowing bins, were pleased when my city finally adopted single-stream recycling, too.

Move forward a couple more years: I was living in Japan, learning to cook vegetables I'd never seen or heard of before that showed up in our farm share box. I was also introduced to two important concepts: *mottainai* and *hara hachi bu*, both of which deeply resonated with me. *Mottainai* is a word that expresses regret regarding wastefulness. In some ways, it's not all that different from the English expression "waste not, want not," but to me it manages to somehow not only capture the shame of wasting a precious resource, but also hold onto the gratitude for what a gift (food, time, money, etc.) it was in the first place. *Hara hachi bu*, an important part of the traditional Okinawan approach to eating, is a phrase that means "eat until you're 80 percent full." In theory that's pretty self-explanatory; in practice I think of it as eating just enough to no longer feel hungry. It's that point where you could keep eating, but maybe don't need to—this way, you're not overindulging and you're giving your brain time to fully process whether you're full before you overdo it.

These three seemingly unrelated life stories actually tell you a lot about me and the origins of this book: I love a good challenge, I hate to see unnecessary waste, and I believe it's important to be conscious of our consumption—of food and beyond. These characteristics set the stage for my love of cooking with scraps.

What Is Cooking with Scraps?

Making the most of your food scraps is a mainstream topic today, and while I'm delighted by the resurgence in enthusiasm for reducing food waste, it's by no means a new topic. People throughout the ages, across lands and cultures, are no strangers to making the most out of what they have—think using chicken bones for stock and stale bread for strata. In 1942, M.F.K. Fisher wrote *How to Cook a Wolf* and inspired readers to cook economically but creatively so as to not feel constrained by wartime shortages. Tamar Adler and Eugenia Bone have tackled kitchen frugality in cookbooks, discussing how using all of an ingredient throughout its lifecycle will not only save you money but will make your food taste better, too. And more recently, chef Dan Barber has popularized kitchen scraps through the Michelin star–worthy meals at his pop-up, wastED.

Cooking with Scraps is a reference work, a book you can turn to when you don't know what to do with underutilized produce parts and other widely neglected odds and ends. What lies unused in one's fridge or pantry is not a purposeless object destined for the waste bin! For the most part, you'll find recipes for the often unused parts—I'm assuming that if you buy carrots you already know how to use the carrot's root, but you might not know how to make use of the greens—every now and then I'll touch on how to incorporate the whole item. For an ingredient to make it into the book, it had to be "worth it" to me as a scrap. For example, when buying broccoli, generally enough of the stem is included that it makes sense to put it to use, but you won't find a recipe focused around ginger peels, because not only does ginger not really need to be peeled (see page 161), but even if you do peel it, you won't generate enough peel at one time to turn into something else. This book is filled with very approachable recipes—simple dishes without long lists of ingredients and overly complicated steps. Cooking with scraps shouldn't be intimidating or overwhelming or feel like a chore: They're *just* ingredients. And the more you cook using these recipes, the more familiar the concepts will become, and you'll realize how easy it is to adapt them to make them your own, swapping in the scraps that you tend to have on hand most often to fit the basic concepts.

On Ingredients and Measurements

Within this book, you'll see short ingredient lists (most are under 10!) with easy-to-find items and measurements in common formats. These were conscious choices designed to keep the recipes accessible to as many people as possible, not intending to frustrate anyone partial to metric measurements. (If you find yourself in need of a metric measurement, you can use the Conversion Tables on page 180.) I, too, enjoy recipes written with metric measurements, especially those for baked goods. However, the vast majority of these recipes simply don't call for that level of precision. I didn't want anyone, especially less experienced home cooks, to be concerned with an exact gram weight when the less precise volume measurement would be more than adequate.

FLOUR

Of course, there's always an exception: One ingredient that can have a big variation if you aren't using metric measurements is flour. I use the fluff-dip-level method of measuring flour, meaning that I use a spoon or a whisk to fluff up the flour right in its bag, then use a spoon or small scoop to dip out the flour and dump it into the measuring cup, and then scrape off the excess with something flat, like the backside of a knife. If I do pull out a scale, 1 cup of all-purpose flour in my kitchen equals 125 grams.

SALT

I have an entire shelf in my kitchen devoted to salts, and the grocery aisle is no less comprehensive than my pantry. For being basically all the same chemically, there are *a lot* of different kinds of salt and switching among them can have a surprisingly large impact on a recipe's outcome. Most of the time I call

for fine-grain sea salt; it's my standard go-to salt. As the name suggests, it's fine-grained, like table salt, but sea salt isn't iodized and treated with additives like table salt often is. For the few cases where I call for kosher salt, a coarser salt than fine-grain sea salt, I'm using Diamond Crystal. A pinch of Diamond Crystal isn't as salty as a pinch of Morton kosher salt (due to the difference in the shape of the grains), so if you have Morton kosher salt on hand, use half the amount called for and adjust to taste. The only other type of salt I'll occasionally call for is a flaky salt, like Maldon or Jacobsen, used as a finishing salt, for example on top of brownies or cookies.

HOT SAUCES

I have almost as many hot sauces as I do salts. The ones I turn to most often are Cholula, Frank's RedHot, Sriracha, and Trader Joe's Yuzu Hot Sauce. Occasionally I'll suggest which hot sauce to use in a recipe, but, really, use whatever you like.

ASIAN INGREDIENTS

I lived in Japan for two years, and complete immersion in Japanese culture had a huge impact on me—and my cooking. Not surprisingly, quite a few Asian ingredients became beloved standards in my kitchen, such as: soy sauce (or tamari), nori (sheets of seaweed), mirin (rice wine), shiso leaves, *shichimi togarashi* (a spice mixture), toasted sesame oil, sushi rice, and more. I'll talk more about these items (and possible substitutions) as they come up in recipes, but for the most part they should be fairly easy to find, if not in the international aisle of a well-stocked grocery store, then at an Asian market, or, if all else fails, ordered online.

OIL

I call for extra virgin olive oil almost exclusively throughout the book. If I'm feeling flush, I'll have a mid-level one for cooking and a higher-end one for drizzling, but most of the time I stick with a mid-level variety that works for both purposes. It has a low smoke point (325° to 375°F), so it isn't the best choice for high-heat cooking (though I don't worry about this too much, and do use it occasionally). For high-heat cooking, I try to keep a neutral-flavored oil on hand with a higher smoke point, like grapeseed or vegetable oil. I also love to use toasted sesame oil and regular sesame oil—the former has a strong toasted sesame flavor and is used in small amounts, while the latter is more neutrally flavored.

BITTERS

You'll find a few recipes for cocktails in these pages, and although none of them calls for bitters, if like me, you enjoy mixed drinks, you likely have a bottle (or a collection) of them in your liquor cabinet. Even if you make cocktails on a semiregular basis, it can take a long time to work your way through a bottle since you're using only a very small amount at a time. I encourage you not to limit your use of bitters to cocktails. A drop or two will liven up club soda or tonic water, but you can take bitters beyond beverages and add a few dashes to a salad dressing or marinade, too.

Food Storage

One step toward reducing waste is to store your food properly so it stays fresh for as long as possible, maximizing the time you have to use it before it spoils. For the most part, pay attention to where something is stored in the grocery store: If it's refrigerated, keep it that way—if not, don't. If you're shopping at the farmers market and aren't sure about the best way to store something, ask a farmer!

A few items benefit from a little extra special treatment:

GREENS

The easiest way to handle greens is to store them in the refrigerator and not wash them until you use them, but you'll likely get a longer life out of them if you either (1) wash them and then store them in the refrigerator loosely wrapped or layered in tea towels (or paper towels) and then placed in a plastic bag or storage container, or (2) wash them in a salad spinner and then store them right in the colander part of the salad spinner in the refrigerator. Both of those options give the greens just enough moisture to keep them fresh without making them more likely to wilt and rot. These suggestions apply to vegetables still sporting their leafy tops, like beets—cut them off and store both parts separately. However you choose to store them, be sure to wash them extremely well as greens can hide a lot of dirt and grit.

HERBS

Soft-stemmed herbs (parsley, basil, chervil, dill, cilantro, and so on) should be treated like a bouquet of flowers—pop them right into a glass of water! I tend to keep all of them out on the counter at room temperature (out of direct sunlight), but if you live in a hot climate, or just have a warm kitchen, they can go in the refrigerator, right in the glass of water, ideally loosely covered with a plastic bag. Use basil as quickly as possible: Out on the counter it might last 3 to 5 days; in the fridge, you'll only get a day or two. The other soft-stemmed herbs should last for 5 to 7 days.

Woody-stemmed herbs (such as rosemary, oregano, and thyme) should be treated more like greens: washed, wrapped in a tea towel (or paper towel), tucked into a plastic bag or storage container, and stored in the refrigerator where they'll be good for a week or two.

BERRIES

Give them a bath in a mix of vinegar and water—I don't measure, I just fill a bowl partway with cool water, add a few glugs of white or apple cider vinegar, and give the berries a dunk. If that makes you nervous, Food52 recommends 1 cup of vinegar for every 3 cups of water. Either way, give your berries a rinse afterward with cool running water to remove any traces of vinegar, then dry them thoroughly and store them in a paper towel–lined storage container.

ONIONS

You probably know that onions should be kept in a cool, dry, and, ideally, dark place. Did you know they'll last even longer if you keep them in nylons (aka pantyhose, depending on your generation)? From Food52er Sam S., I learned that onions can be dropped one at a time into each leg of the nylons—tying a knot after each one—and then hung in a dark spot, like a closet (ideally a closet without clothes and one that guests won't be opening and questioning you about your life choices). This seemingly strange technique maximizes airflow around the onions while simultaneously keeping them separated and moisture-free. Whenever you need an onion, simply snip one off; make sure you're cutting below a knot, so the onion above it stays in place. This method works for any type of onion, but it's especially good for sweet onions, which otherwise are known for having a short shelf life.

POTATOES

Like onions, potatoes should be stored in a cool, dry, dark place, but don't store them with the onions—keeping them together might make your potatoes sprout faster and taste more like onions. Wherever you put them, make sure they have airflow: Either transfer your potatoes to a ventilated container or, if you keep them in the plastic bag they came in, make sure it's well perforated and the top isn't tightly sealed.

CELERY

Keep celery heads whole, wrap them up loosely in aluminum foil, and keep them in the refrigerator crisper drawer as usual. (The plastic bag the celery comes in traps the ethylene it produces, which hastens its vegetal demise.) Aluminum foil isn't the most eco-friendly way to store produce, but it can be reused multiple times to store a few rounds of celery if you're carefully wrapping and unwrapping it. Then, once it starts to shred too much for wrapping celery, go ahead and recycle it.

TOMATOES

Keep tomatoes at room temperature—ideally in a single layer out of direct sunlight. And to keep them fresher longer, store them stem side down while they finish ripening, or cover the stem scar with a piece of tape—either option prevents moisture from leaving the tomato and blocks air, and thus mold and bacteria, from entering the tomato.

If you have fully ripe tomatoes that you just can't eat fast enough, you can refrigerate them and let them come back up to room temperature before eating. Just stick to completely ripe tomatoes, as Harold McGee laid out in his book *On Food and Cooking*. Anything other than fully ripe tomatoes

really suffers in every way after refrigeration—flavor development, coloration, and texture.

BANANAS

Store bananas at room temperature while they ripen, but once they're ripe, it's perfectly fine to put them in the refrigerator. Their skin will darken, but the bananas will stay at the perfect level of ripeness.

The Freezer: Best Practices

For even longer storage, the freezer is your best friend—for scraps and otherwise. (I have an entire shelf devoted to my collection of specialty flours.)

LABEL

Take the time to label what you put in, because although you might think you can tell the difference between two types of pesto, you'll be second-guessing yourself a month from now. I use a permanent marker, like a Sharpie, on zip-top bags, or write with a marker on a piece of masking tape and stick that on a freezer-safe storage container.

USE STORAGE CONTAINERS

I have a number of containers going at all times, one for cheese rinds, one for scraps for stock, one for breadcrumbs, one for croutons, and so on. If everything is well labeled, it is easier for you to find—and use—what you have in there.

WHAT YOU CAN'T FREEZE

The freezer is ideal for preserving a lot of items for months on end, but there are a few things I always avoid freezing. Whole eggs shouldn't be frozen in their shells—if you need to freeze them, crack them and freeze the whites and yolks separately. The texture of raw fruits and vegetables with a high water content (celery, cucumbers, apples, and so on) will be negatively impacted after freezing. Most dairy products and dairy-laden dishes, like cream-based soups, aren't ideal candidates for freezing, either (again, the texture will be compromised; some items will separate after thawing, cheese can become crumbly). Butter is one exception: It freezes really well, and you can also freeze cheese when the change in texture won't be an issue, like Parmesan rinds that are being saved for stock (page 129) or leftover cheese nubs for Cheese Rind Fromage Fort (page 68).

Compost

Even after using every possible part of your food and storing it properly, you're still going to have some food waste. Those scraps don't need to be sent to a landfill; they can be composted to return valuable nutrients to the soil. It's easier than you think to start composting, whether you have a big yard or a postage stamp–size apartment. If a classy compost bin isn't enough to convince you to compost at home, look into what your city has to offer. Some offer compost collection services, others have drop-off programs, and a few even collect "plate scrapings," too—those bits you can't normally compost yourself, like meat and bones.

WHAT

You can compost food waste like fruit and vegetable scraps (the ones you aren't using, of course), eggshells, coffee grounds, tea bags, and nut shells. Don't compost cooked food, dairy products, bones, or fats and oils—they can attract pests and create odor problems. You can also compost things like paper, leaves, hair (when you clean out a hair brush), and grass and other yard clippings. Skip any yard trimmings treated with chemical pesticides, diseased or insect-infected plants, or pet waste—all of which can cause problems in your compost.

WHERE

If you have space to compost outside, you'll need a spot to collect scraps before they make their way out to either a compost pile or bin. I use a small compost bucket with a charcoal filter to help with odor (there really shouldn't be much, if any, anyway), but you could also keep a dedicated container in the freezer if you have the space (and then there's really no chance of offending odors). If you're composting inside, there are special bins you can get at a local hardware store or online.

HOW

Whether you're composting inside or out, you'll want to have an even mix of green material (things like produce scraps and grass clippings) and brown material (things like shredded newspaper and dried leaves). This is important for the compost to be able to develop as well as to ensure there's no unpleasant aroma. You'll need to regularly mix the components of the compost and occasionally add water to keep it moist.

WHY

Since you aren't throwing all of these items away, you're saving space in landfills and reducing your carbon footprint in the process. You're also creating a nutrient-rich product that is wonderful for your soil and can reduce the need for chemical fertilizers.

For more information, including extensive lists covering what (and what not) to compost, visit the EPA's website: epa.gov/recycle/composting-home.

Equipment

I don't have an enormous kitchen, so the tools and appliances that earn a spot in my arsenal need to be truly useful and necessary. This isn't an exhaustive list, but here are a few items you'll find in my kitchen that you might want to add to yours.

FOOD PROCESSOR(S)

I have both a mini food processor and a larger one, and I would strongly recommend getting at least a mini one—it doesn't take up much space, is easy to clean, and comes in handy a lot (like for quickly whipping up a batch of aioli, page 61). I like having both because a full-size one obviously has a larger capacity (great for hummus, page 109), but it also comes with blades that are handy for slicing or shredding lots of vegetables and also for shredding hard cheese (like for Cheese Rind Fromage Fort, page 68).

IMMERSION BLENDER AND/OR BLENDER

Again, I have both, but I use the immersion blender far more often. It's easier to clean (this is a recurring theme for me: the fewer dishes to do, the better) and more flexible, since you can use it to easily puree small amounts of things, and you can also put it directly into a pot and blend a soup without messing with transferring a hot liquid.

STAND MIXER AND/OR HAND MIXER

Another case where you can get by with one or the other (or neither if you're into getting a bonus arm workout every time you want to cream butter and sugar or whip egg whites!). Although it breaks with my predilection for fewer dishes, I've narrowed down to just a stand mixer, as I like the ability to connect other tools to it, like an ice cream maker (see next item).

ICE CREAM MAKER

While it is possible to make ice cream without a dedicated machine, if you think you could get into making it frequently at home, an ice cream maker is worth a purchase. You can get a stand-alone machine or one that works in conjunction with your stand mixer, and either way you'll get a better, smoother texture than you can without it. I have a bowl that works with my stand mixer and I just store it in my freezer, so it's ready to go whenever the ice cream–making urge strikes.

SILICONE BAKING MAT AND/OR PARCHMENT PAPER

These are really helpful to have on hand for recipes that might otherwise stick to a baking sheet (like cookies, page 78, or dried fruit peels, page 5). I have and use both—the silicone baking mat is more environmentally friendly, since you can use it over and over again; the parchment paper provides faster cleanup and is easier if you need to bake multiple ingredients and don't want to wash the silicone between uses.

THERMOMETERS

An oven thermometer is an inexpensive and worthwhile investment that will help you figure out if your oven is accurate (and adjust accordingly based on whether it runs hot or cold). A candy or deep-fry thermometer might not get that much use on a regular basis, but it's helpful when making things like candied citrus peels (page 76) or tempura (page 18), especially if you've never made them before.

MESH STRAINERS

My mesh strainers get a lot of use, and I'd recommend getting more than one, in different sizes. I use them for straining all sorts of things, but I often use them in conjunction with cheesecloth for recipes that need to be finely strained (like nut milks, page 124 or homemade cheese, page 125).

VEGETABLE BRUSH

Hopefully it goes without saying that you should *always* wash (and scrub, when applicable) your produce before eating, but it's especially important when you're cooking with scraps, as you're cooking with parts that are frequently discarded. For example, if you're roasting potato peels, any lingering dirt will ruin the final result—a vegetable brush will help make sure they're as clean as possible.

And, as a brief aside, while washing is important, when you're cooking with scraps it's also wise to make purchasing choices accordingly. For example, pineapples are notorious for being grown using lots of chemicals, so when making Pineapple Peel and Core Lemonade with Mint (page 137), that is one ingredient that I would be sure to buy organic and then scrub the dickens out of with a vegetable brush. If you have produce that seems waxy, it could be a natural waxy coating (like the one apples produce) or food-grade wax (sometimes found on cucumbers, root vegetables, and more). Scrubbing with a brush in warm water will help, but might not remove all of it. Either way, it's safe to eat, but if it bothers you, look for produce without added wax.

Everything in Moderation (Your Best Is Good Enough)

As an avid home cook, I'm preparing meals for my family on a daily basis, and I try to be a conscientious, informed consumer—but I'm far from perfect. I support my local farmers market, and I choose local options when they're available at the grocery store. At the same time, I enjoy bananas, avocados, and coffee—all of which travel a significant distance, which obviously isn't ideal. I try to shop seasonally, but I also have a young daughter with selective eating habits—if I can get her to eat fruit by buying raspberries in January, so be it. I try to buy organic fruits and vegetables (especially when I'm shopping for the worst offenders found on the Environmental Working Group's Dirty Dozen, a shopper's guide to pesticides in produce) or buy from farmers who might not be certified organic but use sustainable growing practices. Sometimes, though, availability and budgets are very real and like many of us, I have to make a few compromises.

It's important to remember that a label can't tell you everything there is to know about your food—there is a wide range of farming practices that can all play a part in helping you to be a responsible eater. When there is a multitude of options, labels can help the informed consumer to make a decision. Even better, strike up a conversation with a farmer the next time you're at the farmers market, and get to know more about how your food is grown.

All of this is to say that grocery choices can get complicated, and, yes, it's perfectly fine to be imperfect—we just need to do the best that we can with what we've got. It's those small changes that add up to make a difference. As with so many things in life, making sustainable choices is a balance, and it's important to work toward finding the balance point that works best for you. I do what I can, and try to make conscientious decisions that fit into my everyday life. And that's because I know that every time I make a purchase it's a vote for what I want to see more of.

I know it can be hard to believe, but changing the food system truly does start in your kitchen. If you're cooking, you're more likely to make wholesome choices and be more connected to your food. And the more you know and care about your food, the more likely you are to eat sustainably. And the more sustainable you are, the less food you waste.

According to the Natural Resources Defense Council, 40 percent of food in the United States goes uneaten, meaning that we are not just wasting food and unnecessarily filling landfills, we are also throwing away the equivalent of $165 billion every year. By making small changes in your own kitchen, you can take steps to make a dent in these statistics.

THE RECIPES

APPLES

Prepping apples for apple pies or a smooth batch of applesauce (or if you happen to live with a picky eater) means piles of peels and cores. Even if you're eating the peels, you'll still always have cores left over. The best way to store them is to freeze them until you accumulate enough to use. I use apple scraps for syrup (page 3), dried apple chips (page 5), and batches of tea that I learned to make from my Food52 colleague Micki Balder. She simmers peels and cores in water with brown sugar, cinnamon, and cloves, but she makes it a little differently every time, so feel free to play around with the basic template—I like mine with a knob of fresh ginger.

These pancakes are thin—more like crepes than what some would consider pancakes. Due to my family's partly Danish heritage, they're what I grew up with, so these are "regular" pancakes to me.

My paternal grandmother—I called her G.G.—would always spread the leftover pancakes with butter (all the way to the edges!), generously sprinkle them with cinnamon sugar, roll them up, and leave them on the counter for people to slice bites off of—you should, too. **SERVES 4**

1. To make the syrup: Place the cores (and peels, if using), the granulated sugar, and the brown sugar in a medium-size saucepan with 1 cup water. Bring the mixture to a boil over medium-high heat, then reduce the heat, and allow the mixture to simmer, stirring occasionally, until the cores are softened and the syrup smells fragrant, 20 to 30 minutes.

2. Strain out the cores and return the syrup to the pan to keep it warm with the residual heat until you're ready to eat. If you'd like it to be thicker, bring it back up to a boil, then reduce the heat, and allow the mixture to simmer until it is reduced and thickened to your liking.

3. To make the pancakes: Meanwhile, place the vinegar and milk in a small bowl and leave it alone for 10 minutes or so—it will curdle in this time.

4. Add the eggs and melted butter to the milk and vinegar mixture in the small bowl and whisk together.

5. Whisk together the flour, baking soda, baking powder, sea salt, and granulated sugar in a medium-size bowl.

6. Whisk the wet ingredients into the dry ingredients until combined; the batter will be very thin.

7. Grease a griddle or cast-iron skillet with a small amount of butter, pour in roughly ⅓ cup of the batter for each pancake, and cook the pancakes over moderate heat. Depending on

DANISH PANCAKES WITH APPLE CORE SYRUP

FOR THE SYRUP

Cores from 5 to 7 apples (and peels, unless you're using them to make chips, page 5), no need to remove the seeds

1 cup granulated sugar

½ cup lightly packed light or dark brown sugar

FOR THE PANCAKES

2 teaspoons apple cider vinegar

2 cups milk (I typically use 2% or whole, but anything other than skim is fine— even nondairy milks)

4 large eggs

¼ cup unsalted butter, melted and cooled slightly, plus more for greasing the skillet and for serving

1 cup all-purpose flour

2 teaspoons baking soda

1 teaspoon baking powder

¼ teaspoon fine-grain sea salt (I do a pinch of salt and a pinch of sugar, but feel free to measure if you'd rather)

¼ teaspoon granulated sugar

Confectioner's sugar or cinnamon sugar, for garnish (optional)

the size of your pan and how much batter you use per pancake, you might only be able to cook one pancake at a time, as the batter spreads quickly. (I use the largest skillet I have and eyeball the amount of batter needed to make a large pancake that fills most of the skillet.) When you see bubbles on the top, and the bottom is golden or light brown, flip the pancake and finish cooking.

8. Repeat Step 7 with all of the remaining batter. Serve immediately: Toss a pancake on someone's plate, smear it with butter, and drizzle with apple core syrup. Dust with confectioner's sugar, if using.

Oven-dried fruit chips are an addictive little snack, and they're easy to customize: Experiment with the spices you use, try cinnamon and nutmeg—or just cinnamon—or skip the spices altogether and just bake the peels straight up. Are you making applesauce? Double the recipe! **MAKES A SNACK FOR A FEW PEOPLE (OR JUST YOURSELF)**

1. Preheat the oven to 250°F.

2. In a medium-size bowl, whisk together the nutmeg, ginger, salt, and sugar. Add the apple peels and toss to coat them with the spice blend.

3. Spread the peels out in a single layer on a parchment- or silicone mat–lined baking sheet and bake for 1 to 2 hours, rotating halfway through. Take them out when they are done to your liking; shorter cooking time will lead to chewier peels, like dried apple rings. If you cook them longer, until the peels are dried out and curling, they will become crispy after cooling, like chips.

4. Let the apple peels cool on the baking sheet before serving. Store at room temperature in an airtight container.

DRIED APPLE PEEL CHIPS

⅛ teaspoon ground nutmeg

⅛ teaspoon ground ginger

Teeny-tiny pinch of fine-grain sea salt

2 teaspoons granulated sugar

Peels from 5 to 7 apples, torn or cut into bite-size pieces, if desired

Try this with pear peels, too. And if you'd rather have a savory snack, try this technique with potato peels and other root vegetable peels, tossing them in a little olive oil or melted butter, adding a sprinkle of salt (and other spices or herbs if you like), and baking until crisp.

AQUAFABA

For the unfamiliar, *aquafaba* is the name for the cooking liquid from beans and other legumes, and it behaves remarkably like egg whites. Aquafaba will whip up into fluffy peaks, whether it comes from canned beans or from soaking and cooking dried beans, but if you're new to the ingredient, I'd start with aquafaba from canned beans. If you have trouble getting the aquafaba to whip at first, don't get discouraged. It does take much longer than whipping egg whites, and I've had some batches fail to whip up at all, but it's worth it to keep trying. When it works, it's a magical ingredient. And if you're *still* having trouble, try a different brand of canned beans. My favorite canned beans are Goya, and it just so happens I've had the best luck with the aquafaba from those beans. You should be able to use low- or no-sodium beans, but if you do, you might need to add a pinch more salt to the recipe.

These brownies are in part modeled after esteemed pastry chef and author Alice Medrich's Best Cocoa Brownies, which I love for their convenience (I almost always have cocoa powder in the pantry) as well as for their fudgy texture—those of you who prefer cakey brownies, I'm sorry, this might not be the recipe for you. I find that I get almost exactly ½ cup aquafaba from one can of beans, and like to use the liquid from black beans for this recipe, though any kind will do. You can find espresso powder online from baking supply stores like King Arthur Flour; I often get Medaglia d'Oro Instant Espresso Coffee at my local grocery store. And if you want to make this vegan, substitute vegan buttery sticks for the butter—it works just as well. **MAKES 16 LARGE OR 25 SMALL BROWNIES**

1. Preheat the oven to 350°F.

2. Line an 8-inch-square baking dish with a parchment sling—two pieces of parchment paper going in opposite directions with an overhang over the edges of the pan—so you can easily lift the brownies out. Alternatively, line the bottom and sides with aluminum foil.

3. Place the aquafaba in the bowl of a stand mixer and whip, using the whisk attachment on medium speed, until the aquafaba gets foamy, and then on medium-high until it gets thick and very foamy, and soft peaks form—10 to 20 minutes. Once you get soft peaks, stop whipping; just as with egg whites, it is possible to overwhip aquafaba and have it deflate.

4. Meanwhile, whisk together the flour, cocoa powder, salt, baking powder, espresso powder (if using), and sugar in a medium-size bowl.

5. Gradually add about half of the combined dry ingredients to the aquafaba, stirring each time to gently combine. Mix in the

FUDGY AQUAFABA BROWNIES

½ cup aquafaba (see page 7 and headnote)

1 cup all-purpose flour

¾ cup natural unsweetened cocoa powder

¼ teaspoon fine-grain sea salt

¼ teaspoon baking powder

½ teaspoon espresso powder (optional, but encouraged)

1¼ cup granulated sugar

½ cup unsalted butter, melted and cooled slightly

1 teaspoon vanilla extract (see page 165)

butter and vanilla extract. Then gradually add the remaining dry ingredients and stir until just combined—it will be a thick batter.

6. Evenly spread the batter in the prepared dish and bake until the brownies look set and the edges are just starting to pull away from the sides of the dish, 30 to 35 minutes.

7. Let cool in the dish, then remove and cut into 16 or 25 squares. Any leftover brownies can be stored at room temperature in an airtight container.

Aquafaba mayonnaise makes a good stand-in for the regular variety in nearly every application (including the recipes in this book—see the next page for a riff on Mexican street corn) and it can be flavored in a variety of ways. I've given you a spicy option (see Variation), but the sky's the limit—play around with other combinations! In the spicy version, you have the option of using Dijon or yellow mustard, but if you plan to use this mayo for the elote (page 13), stick with the yellow mustard. Do note that the final result will be looser than traditional mayonnaise, so it might pool in the bottom of a bowl of potato salad.

In this recipe, I like to use aquafaba from chickpeas or white beans for aesthetic reasons, as the aquafaba from darker beans will be darker in color. **MAKES ABOUT 2 CUPS**

1. Combine the aquafaba, apple cider vinegar, mustard, and salt in the bowl of a stand mixer. Whip, using the whisk attachment on medium speed until the aquafaba gets foamy, and then on medium-high until it gets thick, very foamy, and soft, loose peaks form—10 to 20 minutes. (This could also be done with a hand mixer, or a whisk if you're angling for a serious arm workout.)

2. While the mixer is still running, add ¼ cup of the oil, drop by drop, and then slowly add the remainder of the oil in a thin, steady stream.

3. Transfer the mayonnaise to a covered container, place it in the refrigerator, and allow it to set up slightly before using, about 30 minutes. It will keep in the refrigerator for about 5 days.

AQUAFABA MAYONNAISE

FOR REGULAR MAYONNAISE

¼ cup aquafaba (see headnote)

1 tablespoon apple cider vinegar

1 rounded teaspoon Dijon mustard

½ teaspoon fine-grain sea salt

¾ cup grapeseed oil
(or other neutral-flavored oil)

Substitute 1 tablespoon freshly squeezed lime juice for the vinegar. Stir ¼ teaspoon chili powder, ⅛ teaspoon smoked paprika, and ½ to 1 teaspoon cayenne pepper into the finished mayonnaise (a half teaspoon of cayenne will give it a mild kick—add more if you'd like it to be really spicy).

VARIATION:

SPICY AQUAFABA MAYONNAISE

Elote is a classic Mexican street food: grilled corn that's slathered with mayonnaise, sprinkled with Cotija cheese (and often cilantro), and finished off with lime juice and a dusting of chili powder. This version simplifies the process a little bit, as the Spicy Aquafaba Mayonnaise includes both the lime juice and the chili powder—of course, if you like the visual of the dusting of chili powder, feel free to add it, or a little smoked paprika, just before serving. I think grilling corn with the husk on strikes the perfect balance between getting smoky flavor from the grill and the corn kernels not drying out, but if you have a preferred cooking method, by all means use it. **SERVES 4**

1. Peel back all of the leafy husks of the corn, but don't remove them. Remove all of the silky strands, pull the husks back up, then soak the ears in water for 30 minutes to 1 hour—this ensures the husks won't burn when you grill them.

2. Prepare your grill (as necessary depending on the type) so it will be ready to cook at high heat.

3. When the grill is hot, place the ears of corn, still in their husks, directly on the grill (or right on the hot coals) and cook, turning occasionally, until fully cooked and tender, 10 to 15 minutes. Charred spots are more than okay—they're encouraged.

4. Remove the husks (or leave them on and pulled back as a handle), generously slather each cob with mayonnaise, and then sprinkle with Cotija cheese, cilantro, and chili powder (if using). Serve immediately with lime wedges alongside if you like.

ELOTE WITH SPICY AQUAFABA MAYONNAISE

4 ears corn, with husks

½ cup Spicy Aquafaba Mayonnaise
   (page 11)

½ cup crumbled Cotija cheese
   (or queso fresco)

¼ cup finely chopped cilantro leaves
   (tender stems are okay, too; optional)

Chili powder or smoked paprika,
   for garnish (optional)

Lime wedges, for serving (optional)

Artichokes are an especially delicious spring treat, and I almost always buy them with the intent of devouring the whole thing—bracts (often called the leaves), heart, and stem—with melted butter. But there are times when the hearts might be used for another purpose, and for those times, trimming away everything *but* the hearts can produce a significant pile of scraps. As you've no doubt guessed, the leaves don't need to go to waste. I like to put them to good use in a tasty twist on nachos.

Years ago, food writer and cookbook author Tara Duggan mentioned roasting artichoke leaves, and the idea stuck in my subconscious until recently when I had a dream about artichoke nachos and woke up determined to make them. (Don't make me feel weird—tell me this happens to you, too?) Eat these nachos the way you'd eat a regular artichoke leaf dipped in butter—bite the leaf and scrape off the goodness with your teeth. I don't worry about potential oxidation of the artichoke leaves, so I don't bother coating them in lemon juice—any discoloration will be minor and mainly hidden by the toppings. However, you might want to consider coating the hearts and stems with lemon juice to keep them at their prettiest. **MAKES A SHEET PAN'S WORTH**

1. Bring a large pot of water to a boil and preheat the oven to 375°F.

2. While the water comes to a boil, remove all of the tough outer green leaves from the artichokes. These will be your nachos. Don't rush through this task (you'll risk ripping off the tender, tasty parts at the bottom of the leaves), but don't take the time to sort through them at this point. Stop once you get to the leaves that are directly above the heart, the ones that are a little lighter in color and floppier—they aren't sturdy enough for nachos. (It goes without saying to save the artichoke stems and hearts for another purpose, right? Good.)

3. Add the artichoke leaves to the boiling water and cook until the ends are tender, 8 to 10 minutes. Test one to make sure and then drain them in a colander.

4. While the artichoke leaves are cooking, make the cheater's aioli: With the side of a knife, smash the garlic clove. Sprinkle it with a pinch of sea salt. Alternate chopping and smashing it again with the side of the knife until it turns into garlic paste. Transfer the paste to a small bowl. Whisk in the mayonnaise and lemon juice. Now taste it! This is important, since mayos

ARTICHOKE LEAF NACHOS WITH FETA AND BLACK OLIVES (AND CHEATER'S AIOLI)

4 medium-size artichokes

1 small garlic clove

Fine-grain sea salt

⅓ cup mayonnaise

1 tablespoon freshly squeezed lemon juice

Pinch of granulated sugar, to taste (optional)

2 ounces feta cheese, crumbled (about ½ cup)

2 to 3 ounces sliced black or kalamata olives (⅓ to ½ cup)

Freshly ground black pepper (optional)

½ serrano pepper, sliced (optional)

2 tablespoons coarsely chopped cilantro leaves, for garnish (optional)

are different. If you used a more vinegary one, you might need a pinch of sugar to round it out, or if it needs a little more tang, add a touch more lemon juice.

5. Line a sheet pan with parchment paper (optional, but makes for easier cleanup), and place the artichoke leaves on the pan in a single layer, insides facing up, so they're cup-shaped, ready to hold toppings. Sort through the leaves as you place them, discarding any particularly gnarly-looking ones, or any missing their tender tasty ends.

6. Sprinkle the feta and black olives across the leaves and bake just long enough to heat everything through, letting the feta get soft and a little slumpy, 8 to 10 minutes.

7. Remove from the oven, dollop with the cheater's aioli, and top with black pepper, serrano slices, and cilantro, if desired. Eat, preferably directly from the pan.

Tempura: the Japanese art of transforming vegetables, fish, and shellfish into crispy goodness. What should you tempura? All of your extras and any produce on the verge of going bad , as well as almost any vegetable: asparagus, potatoes, sweet potatoes, green beans, broccoli, cauliflower, onion, carrots, mushrooms, even herbs like shiso leaves or parsley sprigs. If you peel carrots or break off the ends of asparagus, fry those scraps, too! Although vegetable tempura is specified in this recipe, this method works for seafood as well.

If you don't want to invest in two different flours that you don't already have on hand, you can use 1 cup all-purpose flour. When you inevitably fall under the tempura spell, buy the two flours for the next time. I like a light coating of tempura batter, but that's another area to play around with. If you want the coating to be thicker, use a little less club soda.

CRISPY VEGGIE TEMPURA

MAKES ENOUGH BATTER FOR TEMPURA FOR 2 OR 3 PEOPLE AS AN APPETIZER

Canola oil or another neutral-flavored oil with a high smoke point

½ cup cake flour, plus more for dredging (see headnote)

½ cup rice flour

1 large egg yolk

1 cup cold club soda

Vegetable scraps (and non-scraps!) for frying, sliced ⅓ inch thick or less, or chopped into 15 to 20 bite-size pieces

1. Pour the oil into a heavy-bottomed pot to a depth of about 3 inches—less than that, and your ingredients might sink and stick to the bottom rather than properly fry. Heat the oil over medium heat. I aim for it to get to 350°F, but anywhere between 340° and 370°F works. (If you don't have a thermometer, look for the oil to be shimmering, and test the temperature with the method described in the box, opposite). Depending on your cooktop, you might need to adjust the heat down a little to medium-low.

2. While the oil heats, place a cooling rack on top of a baking sheet (to collect excess oil), or set out a layer of paper towels.

3. Whisk the cake flour and the rice flour in a medium-size bowl.

4. Whisk the egg yolk and cold club soda together in a small bowl, then add it to the flour mixture and whisk to combine. Little lumps are okay; don't overmix the batter!

5. Lightly dredge your vegetables in extra cake flour, tapping off any excess, then dip each one in the batter, letting the excess drip off before putting it into the hot oil. You can add several pieces of tempura to the pot at once, but just a few—don't overcrowd. If you're cooking a mix of vegetables and seafood, cook all of the vegetables first, and then the seafood. If you're frying any herbs, skip the flour, and dip one side in batter.

6. Cook like-size items together, as they'll have similar frying times. Delicate herbs will cook in seconds, while firm vegetables, like a slice of sweet potato, will take a few minutes. Once the tempura is puffy and light golden brown, transfer it using tongs (or a spider) to the cooling rack and get other pieces cooking. If you want to make more tempura, use up the first batch of batter and then make another batch. Doubling the recipe will result in gluey tempura.

7. Serve the finished tempura immediately—it does not keep well.

If you don't have a deep-fry thermometer (I recommend getting one—they come in handy!), test the oil by dropping in a small spoonful of batter. It should dip toward the bottom of the pot, but quickly bob back up and start frying.

ASPARAGUS

Young, tender asparagus need not be trimmed at all—its ends are just as enjoyable as the rest of the stalk—but that changes as the season goes on and the asparagus plants get bigger and their stems more fibrous. If you don't want to lose the entire end, sometimes peeling away some of their most fibrous parts is enough to reduce any unpleasant stringiness. As I learned from Food52er Anna G., those trimmings can live their best lives deep-fried (after a quick toss in Wondra flour, a low-protein instant flour, available at well-stocked grocery stores or online) and salted (good luck trying to share). If you do slice or snap off the asparagus's woody ends, the nubs have plenty of flavor left to give to stock (page 129) or pesto.

This recipe is for the ends of middle-of-the-road asparagus: If the ends are extremely woody, they're best saved for stock (page 129). And if the ends don't seem very woody at all, you might just want to peel the ends of your stalks instead, and save those peelings for tempura (page 18)!

This is a thick pesto, meant for tossing with hot pasta or smearing on sandwiches. I also think it would make an excellent dip (maybe mixed with softened cream cheese). Thin it out with additional olive oil to use it as dressing.

Shiso is a Japanese herb in the mint family; I think of it as basil's Asian cousin (basil is also the best substitute should you not be able to find shiso). Look for shiso in the produce section of Asian grocery stores or at your local farmers market. Since it can sometimes be hard to find, I opt to grow my own supply. If you can find shiso leaves, I learned from Food52er Abbie A. that they'll quickly grow roots when their stems are placed in a glass of water on a windowsill. After they do, plant them. I've also grown shiso from seeds procured online and from small plants found at my local farmers market—both options work well. **MAKES ABOUT 1½ CUPS**

CHARRED ASPARAGUS END PESTO

¼ cup plus 1 tablespoon extra virgin olive oil

1- to 2-inch ends cut from the bottom of 1 bunch of asparagus

1 cup loosely packed fresh shiso or basil leaves (see headnote)

½ cup pine nuts, toasted (see Note)

1 garlic clove, minced

½ cup finely grated pecorino Romano cheese

1 tablespoon freshly squeezed lemon juice

1. In a medium-size heavy skillet, heat 1 tablespoon of the oil over medium-high heat. Add the asparagus ends to the hot pan, and let them cook, undisturbed, until the side touching the pan chars, 3 to 5 minutes. Move them around a bit to expose another side to the heat, and let them cook, undisturbed, until they are charred on all sides and can be easily pierced with a knife, another 3 to 5 minutes. Remove from the pan and let cool slightly.

2. Using a knife, finely chop the asparagus ends. This is important: If you try to skip this step, the food processor will shred the cooked ends and you'll have stringy pesto.

3. Add the chopped asparagus ends, shiso, pine nuts, and garlic to a mini food processor and pulse to process all ingredients, scraping down the bowl a couple of times as needed. Then add the cheese and lemon juice and pulse a few more times. Finally, add the rest of the olive oil and process again until smooth. The pesto is at its best when used immediately, so the basil doesn't discolor, but can be stored in an airtight container in the refrigerator or freezer.

NOTE: I like to toast nuts and seeds in a dry skillet over medium heat, stirring or shaking the pan occasionally. Different items will have different toasting times, so don't walk away from the pan unless you like your toasted nuts on the burnt side.

For a larger quantity, heat the oven to 350°F, spread the seeds or nuts in a single layer on a baking sheet, and bake until golden brown. Again, cooking times will vary, so keep a close eye on them.

Every Saturday morning, my family kicks off our weekend with a trip to the farmers market and Zingerman's, an Ann Arbor institution that began with a delicatessen and has now expanded to an entire community of businesses—including mail order, so you, too, can enjoy a little Zingerman's wherever you may be. We visit the former for fruits and vegetables, of course, and the latter for bread and cheese. One day, my husband noticed that Zingerman's meat counter had bacon ends for sale and asked if I could do something with them—I was only too happy to experiment. Bacon ends are exactly what they sound like—the end pieces (larger chunks or smaller chips) of a slab of bacon that are too small to be sliced into strips. Your butcher might not have bacon ends out on display, but they'll almost certainly be willing to sell them to you. If not, just substitute a couple of slices of bacon.

BACON-Y TOMATO JAM

1 bacon end, from a smoky
 type of bacon if possible
 (a thick end slice, not the little
 chipped pieces—see page 23)
1 medium-size white or yellow onion,
 chopped
3 pounds tomatoes (7 to 8 medium-size
 tomatoes, cored and chopped—
 about 7 cups)
¼ cup maple syrup (any grade except
 the very darkest)
¼ cup lightly packed dark brown sugar
1 cup granulated sugar
¼ cup apple cider vinegar
1 teaspoon fine-grain sea salt
1 teaspoon yellow mustard seeds
Freshly squeezed lemon juice (optional)

My introduction to tomato jam came via longtime Food52er (and blogger and cookbook author) Jennifer Perillo's sweet and savory version with coriander and cumin. I was skeptical: Would it be like ketchup? Super sweet jam? It turns out to be neither. Hers neatly walks the line between sweet and savory, and this one does, too, with the addition of a bacon end for a pleasantly smoky flavor. I like tomato jam on grilled cheese sandwiches, but try it on other types of sandwiches, too, or use it as a spread with cheese and crackers. **MAKES 2 TO 3 CUPS**

1. Add the bacon end, onion, tomatoes, maple syrup, dark brown sugar, granulated sugar, apple cider vinegar, sea salt, and mustard seeds to a large, nonreactive pot (see Note) over medium heat. Give it all a good stir and cook, stirring every so often, lowering the heat as you go if it seems like it's bubbling and splattering too much, until the mixture cooks down to a thick, jammy consistency. Depending on how juicy your tomatoes are, this could take as little as 45 minutes to as much as 3 hours. Remove the bacon and discard; it's done its job!

2. At this point, if you're happy with the slightly chunky consistency, you're done. I like my tomato jam a little smoother, so I use an immersion blender to puree it all up a bit. This could also be done at the beginning, before cooking—and before adding the bacon!—but I like to wait until the end so I can clearly see the finished consistency. Taste to see if it needs a bit more salt or a squeeze of lemon juice to brighten it up, and adjust accordingly.

3. Store in glass jars (or similar covered containers) in the refrigerator for up to 2 weeks, or freeze for longer storage.

NOTE: Nonreactive cookware is made of a material that won't react with acidic ingredients—like stainless steel, glass, ceramic, and enamel-coated metal. Using reactive cookware—like copper or aluminum—with acidic ingredients not only could result in discolored pots and pans, but the food could also pick up a metallic taste.

If you're surprised to have come to a section on using scraps from everyone's favorite yellow fruit, you're not alone—the peels seem like they're best used in a comedy skit. But banana scraps *are* edible and can be cooked down and pureed into a paste that's not tough or rubbery at all (try using it in muffins or other baked goods). The magic of the cake recipe on page 26 is that no one will guess it's made with banana peels unless you want to fess up (although honesty may be the best policy—see the note on page 27). When repurposing your peels, use brown-freckled ones from very ripe bananas—the kind of bananas you might mash up for banana bread. Using peels from eating-ripe-but-not-*really*-ripe bananas will work, but you'll get less of a pronounced banana flavor. As always, when eating the typically discarded outer layers of produce, choose organic if possible, and scrub well.

BANANA PEEL CAKE WITH BROWN SUGAR FROSTING

FOR THE CAKE

Peels from 2 very ripe bananas,
   stem and very bottom discarded
   (see Note)

½ cup unsalted butter, softened, plus
   more for buttering the pans

1½ cups granulated sugar

2 large eggs, separated

½ cup buttermilk

1⅔ cups cake flour, plus more flour
   (any type) for flouring the pans

1 teaspoon baking soda

¼ teaspoon baking powder

½ teaspoon fine-grain sea salt

FOR THE FROSTING

½ cup unsalted butter

1 cup packed light or dark brown sugar

¼ cup milk, 2% or higher

1¾ to 2 cups powdered sugar, sifted

This cake is loosely adapted from my paternal grandmother G.G.'s banana cake recipe. Well, I think of it as my grandmother's recipe, but it was actually her mother's or her mother-in-law's . . . either way, it lasted through the generations for a reason. It was a special cake that she would make for my father's birthday, as it's his favorite cake (and mine, too). The major difference between this cake and hers? Mine is made with banana peels (yes, really) instead of bananas. It's a simple-seeming cake (no vanilla?! not a spice to be found?!), but it tastes just like your favorite banana bread. **MAKES ONE 2-LAYER CAKE**

1. Preheat the oven to 350°F.

2. To make the cake: Cut the banana peels into 1-inch pieces and place them in a small saucepan with 1 cup water. Bring to a boil over medium-high heat, then reduce the heat and simmer for 10 minutes. Remove the pan from the heat and allow the mixture to cool slightly, then drain the banana peels, reserving ¼ cup of the cooking water.

3. Meanwhile, butter and flour the sides of two 8-inch round cake pans and line the bottoms with parchment paper. Butter and flour the pans again to coat the paper.

4. Transfer the peels and the ¼ cup of cooking water to a tall, narrow container and puree with an immersion blender until completely smooth (a mini food processor would do the trick, too!).

5. Cream together the butter and sugar in a large bowl using an electric mixer (or a wooden spoon for an arm workout) until pale and fluffy, 3 to 5 minutes. Add the egg yolks one at a time, mixing until incorporated, and scraping down the sides of the bowl after each addition. Mix in the banana peel mixture, then stir in the buttermilk until well combined.

6. In a medium-size bowl, whisk together the flour, baking soda, baking powder, and salt. Add the dry ingredients to the bowl with the butter mixture and stir gently, just until combined.

7. Put the egg whites in another bowl (make sure it's clean and dry!) and whisk until soft peaks form—either by hand or with the whisk attachment on an electric mixer. If using an electric mixer, start slowly and gradually increase speed to medium-high. You'll know you're done when you pull out the whisk or beater and a soft peak is formed, but immediately collapses. Gently fold the egg whites into the batter and divide the batter evenly between the two prepared pans.

8. Bake, rotating the pans halfway through, until the tops are golden and a toothpick inserted into the center of each cake pulls out with dry crumbs rather than wet batter, about 25 minutes. Let the cakes cool completely in the pans.

9. When the cakes are completely cool and you're ready to assemble, make the frosting. Melt the butter in a medium saucepan over low heat. Stir in the brown sugar and cook, stirring constantly, for 2 minutes. Stir in the milk, raise the heat to medium-high and cook, stirring constantly until the mixture boils. Remove from the heat, and let cool until lukewarm. Gradually whisk in 1¾ cups powdered sugar, beating until smooth. Add the additional ¼ cup powdered sugar if the frosting is too loose. Use the frosting immediately, as it will begin to thicken and stiffen as it sits.

10. To remove the cake from the pans, invert one cake pan on a serving plate, lift off the pan, and peel off the parchment. Repeat for the second cake pan. Put one layer of the cake on a serving platter and spread about one third of the frosting evenly over the top. Set the other layer on top, and spread the remaining frosting over the top and sides of the cake.

NOTE: Banana peels contain some of the same proteins found in latex, and could cause an allergic reaction. Those same proteins might also make your immersion blender feel slightly gummy to the touch. Rub the surface down with cooking oil before cleaning it, and then wash it normally.

BEETS

I'm embarrassed to admit it, but when I first began grocery shopping for myself, the tops of root vegetables—radish greens, turnip greens, beet greens—consistently went to waste. Not because I forgot to store them properly, which is to separate the greens from the roots (see page xix), but rather because I didn't use them at all. It makes me cringe to think of it: I was throwing away food that was not only good for me but delicious, too. Luckily I've since learned the error of my ways and now know that all of those greens can easily be added to soups and stews (at the last minute, so they wilt just a bit), omelets, hashes, or nearly any skillet meal; or sautéed and enjoyed as a side dish or as a pizza topping (page 30). And though you risk temporarily turning your hands (and seemingly every surface in your kitchen) a vibrant shade of pink every time you peel beets, it will be well worth it if you're saving those peels to infuse tequila (page 150).

The title of this recipe might say "beet greens," but this method can be used for any greens from root vegetables, as well as for other greens like kale, collards, and Swiss chard. The recipe is very flexible, but try starting with one substantial bunch of greens, like from a medium-size bunch of beets or turnips, or two to three smaller bunches, like from radishes. **MAKES A SMALL SIDE DISH FOR 2**

1. Separate the stems from the leaves. Tear any large leaves into smaller pieces, and finely chop the stems (unless you're reserving them for another use, like pickling).

2. Heat the olive oil in a sauté pan over medium heat. Add the shallot and garlic to the pan along with a pinch of sea salt and cook until softened, but not browned, 3 to 5 minutes.

3. Add the chopped stems, and sauté until softened, stirring occasionally, for another 10 minutes or so, depending on the type of stems and how finely you chopped them.

4. Add the greens to the pan. If you have so many greens they threaten to overflow the pan, add them in batches. Once the first batch starts to wilt and cook down, add the next (see note).

5. Cook until the greens are fully softened and wilted. If you're using them in another recipe, like Beet Greens and Eggplant Pizza (page 30) or a frittata (page 122), stop here. If you're serving them as a side dish, add a squeeze of lemon juice (start with a tablespoon or two and adjust to taste), or a sprinkle of red pepper flakes—or both!

NOTE: If you're cooking really sturdy greens like kale or collards, consider adding 2 tablespoons of water to the pan (and covering it) to partially steam the greens, speeding up the cooking process.

BASIC, SAUTÉED BEET GREENS

1 medium-size to large bunch greens with stems (no need to dry the greens after washing, any residual water will help steam them)

2 tablespoons extra virgin olive oil

1 medium-size shallot, finely chopped (about 2 tablespoons)

2 garlic cloves, minced

Fine-grain sea salt

Freshly squeezed lemon juice, for serving (optional)

Red pepper flakes, for serving (optional)

BEET GREENS AND EGGPLANT PIZZA

1 smallish eggplant (about 12 ounces),
  cut into ½-inch slices

½ cup extra virgin olive oil, plus more
  (optional) for greasing a baking sheet

½ teaspoon fine-grain sea salt

¼ teaspoon freshly ground black pepper

8 ounces to 1 pound pizza dough
  (see headnote)

Cornmeal, for dusting the pizza stone

½ batch (about ¾ cup) of Basic Sautéed
  Beet Greens (page 29)

5 ounces pepper Jack cheese, grated

When I first started making pizza at home, I quickly learned that most of the time, it's better not to go overboard on the toppings. But then I tried a Grilled Eggplant and Olive Pizza from Deb Perelman of Smitten Kitchen, and despite the fact that I was unsure of (1) a very topping-heavy pizza, and (2) eggplant on pizza, I fell in love and worked it into my regular dinner rotation. This pizza is a scraps-focused homage to Perelman's pizza.

Eggplant haters: I implore you to give this a shot. The grilled eggplant almost melts on the pizza, creating creamy bites that eliminate the need for sauce. But if you try it and still insist: Swap out the eggplant, keep the beet greens, and try cooked ground sausage instead. Or make a breakfast pizza—use more beet greens and crack a few eggs on top before baking.

A note on the dough: If you're making your own (I'm fond of the recipes from Roberta's restaurant in Bushwick, Brooklyn, and the no-knead dough that Jim Lahey of Sullivan St. Bakery made famous—a quick internet search will bring them up), you can stick to a smaller 8-ounce ball. However, if you're buying premade dough at the store, I think it's easiest to use a larger amount. Premade dough is convenient, but doesn't seem to stretch out as well. **MAKES ONE 12-INCH PIZZA**

1. Preheat your oven to its highest bake setting, 500° or 550°F, with a rack in the lowest position. Set a pizza stone or baking steel, if you have one, on the rack to preheat it.

If you do have a pizza stone or a baking steel, you'll get better results by heating the stone or steel in the oven for up to an hour ahead of time. This means you'll need to be extra careful handling a piping hot stone, or employ a pizza peel. Of course, if you own the latter, you've probably got your pizza-making technique down pat. Carry on.

2. Place the eggplant slices in a medium-size bowl. Slowly drizzle them with the olive oil, tossing as you go, using your hands to make sure both sides of each slice get evenly coated, and then toss the slices with the salt and pepper.

3. Cook the eggplant slices on a grill pan over medium heat until tender, 6 to 8 minutes, flipping midway through. Set aside to cool slightly, and then cut into bite-size pieces.

4. Stretch the dough out into a roughly 12-inch circle. I like to lightly flour my hands and, going around the outside of the ball, pinch the dough between the base of my palm and my fingers, allowing gravity to help stretch the dough. Once the dough has stretched to larger-than-hand-size, I start smacking it from one hand to the other, doing a quarter turn between each transfer (this is a technique I've held onto from shaping focaccia in a bakery). If that seems too complicated, lightly flour the ball and the countertop and stretch it out with your hands (fingertips or knuckles both work well) or a rolling pin.

5. Carefully remove the preheated pizza stone or baking steel from the oven, lightly sprinkle it with cornmeal, and transfer the dough to it. If you don't have a pizza stone or baking steel, a baking sheet is fine—flip it over so you don't have to deal with the sides, and grease it with additional olive oil.

6. Top the dough with the eggplant, beet greens, and cheese. Bake until the crust is well browned, 8 to 12 minutes. Serve hot, cut into slices.

BEET PEEL MARGARITA

Kosher salt

1 ounce Cointreau or other
orange-flavored liqueur

2 limes, halved and juiced
(don't discard the spent limes)

3 ounces Beet Peel Tequila
(page 150)

4 teaspoons simple syrup
(see box)

Additional lime slices, for garnish
(optional)

One of my favorite restaurants in my hometown of Grand Rapids, Michigan, has a beet margarita on their menu, made with pickled beet juice. Since I don't get there as often as I'd like, I had to find a way to re-create it at home. I first played around with a freshly juiced version, but then I found that using beet peel–infused tequila (page 150) was an even better way of imparting the earthy beet flavor to the drink without watering it down. Your eagle eyes may pick up that I call for 4 teaspoons of simple syrup here instead of 1 tablespoon plus 1 teaspoon. Listing the ingredients in this way means you just have to be able to count to 4 (1 for Cointreau, 2 for lime juice, 3 for tequila . . .) and you're well on your way to a delicious margarita! **MAKES 2 COCKTAILS (SHARING IS OPTIONAL)**

1. Pour some kosher salt into a small, shallow dish.

2. Add the Cointreau, lime juice, tequila, and simple syrup to a shaker filled with ice.

3. Run the spent lime halves around the rims of two glasses (or one, no judgment), dip the rims of the glasses in the salt, and then fill the glasses with ice.

4. Shake the cocktail until chilled and then strain into the glasses. Garnish with a slice of lime, if desired.

Simple syrup is nothing more than sugar and water. Combine equal measures of water and granulated sugar in a small saucepan over medium heat and cook, stirring occasionally, until the sugar dissolves. Remove from heat and let cool before using. Transfer any extra to a glass jar or similar container and store it in the refrigerator for up to 2 weeks.

BEET GREENS SALAD WITH WARM GOAT CHEESE ROUNDS

FOR THE SALAD

1 package (5 ounces) plain goat cheese

⅓ cup all-purpose flour

1 large egg

½ cup panko or fine breadcrumbs (page 39)

Grapeseed oil or extra virgin olive oil, for pan-frying

2 bunches beet greens, leaves only, finely shredded (see headnote)

FOR THE DRESSING

1 tablespoon balsamic vinegar

¼ cup extra virgin olive oil

Pinch of fine-grain sea salt

Freshly ground black pepper

Most of the time I think we gravitate toward cooking sturdier greens like Swiss chard or beet greens, but we don't have to, because they're good raw as well. If you haven't shredded greens before, think of it like a basil chiffonade (only bigger): Stack leaves on top of one another, gently roll them up, and then slice across the rolled leaves. You'll end up with ribbons of greens; the closer together your cuts are, the thinner your strips will be—that matters much more for a basil chiffonade than for a salad, which doesn't need to be all that precise. If you only have one bunch of beet greens, or the bunches seem small, add in another sturdy green, like spinach. You want to have 6 to 8 ounces of greens. **SERVES 3 OR 4**

1. Place the goat cheese in the freezer for 15 minutes; it will be easier to slice in the next step.

2. Slice the goat cheese into rounds. I like to do 6 slices, so if you're serving three people, they'll each get two rounds. If you're serving four, slice the log into 4 thick slices so no one gets shorted.

3. Set up three bowls for coating the goat cheese rounds. Put the flour in the first bowl; the egg, lightly beaten with a teaspoon or two of water, in the second bowl; and the panko in the third.

4. Pour the oil into a small or medium-size pan—you want the bottom of the pan to be generously covered in oil, about ¼ inch deep—and place the pan over medium heat.

5. Coat each goat cheese round first in flour, then egg, and then the panko—I like to keep one hand dedicated to flour and the other hand for the egg and panko to try to contain the mess. Place the coated rounds aside on a plate.

6. Once the oil has heated up, place the goat cheese rounds in the oil. Cook them on the first side until they're light brown and crispy, 1 to 2 minutes, then flip and cook them on the other side for 30 to 45 seconds—they should be uniformly crispy and lightly browned. The medium heat level is important; a gentle ring of bubbles should form around each round as you put it in the oil. If the oil is too hot, the cheese will

start oozing before the panko has crisped up, so if the oil bubbles furiously when you put the cheese in, turn down the heat a little. When the rounds are done, transfer them to a cooling rack or a paper towel to drain any excess oil.

7. Whisk together the balsamic vinegar, extra virgin olive oil, sea salt, and a grind of pepper in a medium-size bowl. Add the shredded greens and toss to coat. Taste and adjust for salt and pepper as needed.

8. Divide the greens among plates and top each serving with the warm goat cheese rounds.

NOTE: If you haven't used all of the beets yet, they can be added to the salad. I follow Food52 founder Amanda Hesser's technique for roasting beets (who in turn got it from chef Tom Colicchio) in foil packets: Heat your oven to 350°F. Place the beets on a piece of aluminum foil on a baking sheet, drizzle them with olive oil, and season with salt and pepper. Fold the foil over to create a packet and crimp the edges together on all three open sides. Bake until the beets are tender, 30 to 60 minutes. Let them cool in the packet. When they're cool enough to touch, peel off the skins with your fingers, cut the beets into slices or wedges, and add them to the salad.

Strata.

Much like the Oven Frittata (page 122), a strata is a versatile dish for clearing out odds and ends in the fridge, and it's make-ahead friendly.

In the interest of full disclosure: I could easily pass on stuffing, bread pudding, french toast—you get the idea. So why on earth would I tell you to make a strata? Well, for starters, I've met very few people who share my indifference to mildly mushy bread-focused dishes, so the odds are good that you enjoy them, too. But secondly, a strata is one of the best ways to put stale bread to good use. So even though they aren't my favorite, they still make a regular appearance at my house, because I love bread, and I don't always finish it before it gets stale. I normally use a 3-quart casserole dish for a strata, which makes enough for 4 to 6 servings, and plan to use 6 to 8 cups of cubed (¾ to 1 inch) stale bread. You can use any size dish you choose though; toss in the bread cubes as you cut them until it's mostly—but not all the way—full, then measure how much you have and adjust the egg-and-milk ratio accordingly.

ANY-SEASON STRATA

MAKES 4 TO 6 SERVINGS

Butter for greasing the baking dish, plus more (optional) for sautéing the filling

6 large eggs

1¼ cups milk (for an eggier strata, up the amount of eggs; for a mushier strata, add more milk)

Fine-grain sea salt and pepper, to taste

Up to 6 cups uncooked or 3 cups cooked vegetables and meat for the filling (see Step 3)

Olive oil, for sautéing the filling (unless using butter)

6 to 8 cups cubed (¾ to 1 inch) stale bread (see Note)

¾ to 1½ cups grated or crumbled cheese, depending on how many cheese nubs you're trying to clear out (and how cheesy you want it to be)

1. Grease a 3-quart baking dish with butter.

2. Whisk the eggs and milk together along with a healthy pinch of salt and a few grinds of pepper, and set aside.

3. Vegetables and meat need to be cooked before baking, so chop any uncooked items and sauté them with a little butter or olive oil. The amounts you choose can vary widely, and remember that most will shrink after cooking, so it's hard to overdo it. A small or medium onion and a garlic clove or two are always a good start, and then think about what you have left in your fridge that might work well together. A half pound of sausage and a bunch of spinach (cook the sausage first, and then add the greens to wilt them), or a package of mushrooms with bacon and Swiss cheese, or leftover squash with a small bunch of Swiss chard, or cherry tomatoes with corn cut off of a couple of cobs and blobs of ricotta. (Note that leftover cooked meats and vegetables don't need to be cooked again.)

4. Spread about half the bread cubes in the bottom of the buttered dish, then layer on half of the cheese and half of the vegetables and meat. Then repeat: Layer on the rest of the bread and remaining ingredients.

5. Pour the egg and milk mixture over everything. Cover and refrigerate for at least 30 minutes or up to 1 day.

6. Preheat the oven to 350°F. Remove the dish from the refrigerator and bake, covered with aluminum foil, for 30 to 40 minutes. Uncover at the end for some browning action if desired.

NOTE: If your bread isn't stale to start with, you have a couple of options for getting it there. If you're not in a rush, place thick slices of bread on a baking sheet or for even better air circulation, a cooling rack, and leave the slices to dry out for a day. The faster option involves your oven. I pop cubes of bread on a baking sheet in a 200°F oven and leave them in there while I prep other ingredients—they will dry out in about 40 minutes or so. If you want them to dry even faster, crank it up to 350°F, but pay closer attention—your bread cubes will be toasted in 15 to 20 minutes.

The best thing since sliced bread? Stale bread.

Writing about reducing food waste has expanded my cooking horizons and has made me more comfortable with all sorts of potential scraps. But it's also been a personal journey in learning to love stale bread. I went from being skeptical of any vaguely mushy use for day-old bread to willingly putting it in different dishes—and liking them. You can use it to make breadcrumbs, which can be crisped in a skillet and form a bed for fried eggs (page 41), sprinkled on pasta (page 99), used to add texture to salads and roasted vegetables, or to bulk up meatballs or savory cakes (think crab cakes or bean burgers), and on and on. Or use it to make croutons, French toast, stuffing, or a strata. When I'm on top of my game, I like to freeze it in its final form, taking the time to turn it into breadcrumbs or cubes. But if you don't have time, go ahead and freeze it as is—you can figure it out when you thaw it.

FRESH BREAD-CRUMBS

Despite the name of this recipe, most often I use bread that is not superfresh to make breadcrumbs, because I'd rather use bread that's becoming stale for this purpose. A baguette or rustic artisanal loaf of bread works best for this; smooshy sandwich-style loaves from the grocery store aren't the best bet, but will work in a pinch. Once you have your bread, you have several options for turning it into breadcrumbs:

Use your fingers. Tear it into whatever size pieces you'd like (as I call for in Crispy Breadcrumb Fried Eggs, page 41). Stick with this method if your bread is really soft.

Use a grater. Any size will work, but of course the size you use—whether the largest holes on a box grater or a Microplane—will determine the size of the breadcrumbs you end up with.

Use a food processor. I prefer to use the grating disk, but the chopping blade will work, too, if you're okay with breadcrumbs of varying sizes.

If a recipe calls for dried breadcrumbs, put them on a baking sheet in a 300°F oven until they are just ever so slightly golden brown. The time will vary depending on the amount of breadcrumbs baking at once. If I only need a small amount, I'll put them in a dry pan on the stovetop over medium heat and move them around with a spatula every so often, again until just barely golden in color.

ADDICTIVELY CRUNCHY CROUTONS

As with breadcrumbs, ideally I like to make croutons with sturdy bread that isn't super fresh. Cut (or tear) the bread into crouton-size pieces (whatever that may mean to you) and toss them in enough olive oil or melted butter to coat them. If desired, at this point season them with salt and pepper, or spices, or a sprinkling of seeds, and toss again. Cook the croutons in a 375°F oven until crunchy and golden brown, 5 to 10 minutes—if you're making a large batch, keep checking every 5 minutes after that.

These eggs are exactly what they sound like: fried eggs combined with teeny croutons. I like them on top of vegetables or rice bowls. You can add a sprinkling of herbs like dill to the pan, but not too much while you're cooking the eggs—you don't want to introduce excess water. As written, this recipe makes fried eggs with little salty, crunchy breadcrumb bits embedded in them. If you want to go breadcrumb-crazy, or if you have more than one slice to use up, tear up 2 or 3 slices of bread. In Step 4, you'll need to scooch the breadcrumbs aside in spots to make little nests that you can crack the eggs into. **SERVES 2 TO 4**

CRISPY BREAD-CRUMB FRIED EGGS

1½ tablespoons unsalted butter

1 slice stale bread, torn into small (pea-size or smaller) breadcrumbs

Fine-grain sea salt

4 large eggs

Freshly ground black pepper

Hot sauce (optional)

1. Melt the butter in a medium-size skillet over medium heat.

2. Add the breadcrumbs to the melted butter and stir them around to coat. Add a pinch of salt or season to taste.

3. Cook the breadcrumbs until golden brown and crisp, 3 to 4 minutes.

4. Make sure the breadcrumbs are scattered evenly in the skillet and then crack the eggs on top of them.

5. Continue cooking the eggs over medium heat until the whites are set and the yolks are cooked to your liking, and season with sea salt. This could take just over a minute or up to 4 minutes depending on your yolk preferences. I like my fried eggs over-easy, with the yolk still runny, so once the whites are almost completely set, I flip them over briefly to set the other side, and flip them back again for plating—solely for aesthetic reasons.

6. Sprinkle with salt and pepper, and optionally, a few dashes of hot sauce.

There are no bad food scraps … some are just

more versatile than others. Like broccoli stalks. They're one of the best. (Don't tell them I said so, though. I think that's akin to choosing a favorite child, and all scraps are special little stars!) The florets are the prized part of broccoli, much like they are in cauliflower, and the large main stalk and little stem pieces are sometimes discarded after they're cut off. Don't do that! Peel off the thick outer layer of skin, and shave or grate the stems to use in salads and slaws or cut them into batons for crudités or twirling (kidding, that's a different kind of baton). Broccoli stems can be sautéed, poached, or grilled, too. And thanks to Food52er Marina C., I learned that the longer, woody stems of later-season broccoli have the unique ability to be treated like bones—steam them, split them in half, and scoop out the tender "marrow" in the center.

This is a bowlful of comfort—like an adult version of macaroni and cheese, only one for those times when powdered cheese just won't cut it—and it comes together really quickly, making it a good weeknight dinner option to work into your rotation. **SERVES 3 OR 4 AS A MAIN DISH**

1. Heat the olive oil in a medium-size saucepan over medium heat. Add the onion and cook until nearly translucent, 5 to 7 minutes. Add the sausage and cook until lightly browned, stirring occasionally and breaking up any large clumps, about 10 minutes. Turn the heat to low once you're done.

2. Meanwhile, fill a large pot with salted water (see box, page 87) and bring it to a boil over high heat.

3. Add the tortellini to the boiling water and cook according to package directions, adding the broccoli pieces to the water with about 5 minutes left to go. (This results in broccoli that still has a little tooth to it; if you'd like very soft broccoli, allow for more cooking time.)

4. Drain the pasta and broccoli, reserving ½ cup of the cooking water.

5. Add the pasta and broccoli to the pan with the sausage and onions. Add the cream, grated cheese, and about half of the pasta water, stirring to combine. Add the remaining water if the mixture seems too dry. Season to taste with salt and pepper if desired (between the sausage and the cheese, you probably won't need much—if any!).

NOTE: If you'd rather, instead of two broccoli stems, you can use one whole head of broccoli (florets and stem). Florets can be chopped slightly larger than stem pieces—though they should still be bite-size.

CHEESE TORTELLINI WITH SAUSAGE AND BROCCOLI STEMS

1 tablespoon extra virgin olive oil

1 medium-size onion, diced (about 1 cup)

½ pound sweet or hot Italian sausage, removed from casing

1 package (10 to 14 ounces) cheese tortellini

2 broccoli stems, peeled to remove the tough outer layer (see Step 1, page 45) and chopped into ½-inch pieces (see Note)

¼ cup heavy whipping cream or half-and-half

⅔ cup finely grated pecorino Romano cheese

Fine-grain sea salt and freshly ground black pepper, to taste

This dish came about because I was craving chickpeas (Don't judge, they're my desert island food—I really love chickpeas.) and I was thinking about British chef April Bloomfield's Lemon Caper Dressing, an extraordinarily lemony dressing that makes your mouth pucker in the most wonderful way.

The perfect scrap to marry those two thoughts had to be broccoli stems: They provide a complementary flavor, are an excellent vehicle for soaking up the lemony dressing, and I just love how little broccoli stem coins look mixed in with the chickpeas. (What can I say, they're cute!) **MAKES APPETIZERS FOR A SMALL CROWD OR A SINGLE SLICE OF TOAST EACH FOR 3 OR 4**

1. Remove the tough outermost layer of the broccoli stems, reserving any leaves. I like to use a paring knife to get it started and then I just peel it away. Once it's all peeled, chop the broccoli into roughly chickpea-size pieces.

2. Heat ⅓ cup olive oil in a medium-size saucepan over medium heat. Add the broccoli. If the pieces aren't fully covered, add the remaining olive oil. Cook until nearly tender, about 5 minutes, depending on the size of your pieces.

3. Add the chickpeas, 3 tablespoons of the lemon juice, and the salt. Cook until the broccoli is fully cooked, but not yet turning to mush, another minute or two, and remove from the heat. Add the broccoli leaves and stir, so that they wilt. Taste

....

For some dishes (like hummus, page 109), I think it makes a big difference to start with dried chickpeas. For others, like this one, canned chickpeas will work just fine, as long as they're good ones—hard, mealy chickpeas can ruin a dish. I like to use Goya.

....

LEMONY OLIVE OIL– POACHED BROCCOLI STEMS AND CHICKPEAS ON RICOTTA TOAST

Stems (large and small) and leaves from
    2 heads broccoli
⅓ to ½ cup extra virgin olive oil, plus
    more for drizzling
1 can (15 ounces) chickpeas, drained and
    rinsed (see box, bottom, and Note,
    page 46)
¼ cup freshly squeezed lemon juice
½ teaspoon fine-grain sea salt
Thick slices of crusty bread
    (use a baguette if you're making
    this as an appetizer, or 3 or 4 slices
    from a larger artisanal loaf like
    sourdough if you're serving it to
    a few)
1 container (16 ounces) ricotta cheese
    (you won't use all of it, but the
    amount you'll need will vary
    depending on whether you're
    making this for a few or many)
Red pepper flakes, for garnish (optional)

and adjust, adding the additional tablespoon of lemon juice or more salt if necessary.

4. Meanwhile, toast the bread slices in a toaster (or on a sheet pan under the broiler).

5. Spread some ricotta cheese on each piece of toast (I like a nice thick layer) and then top each one with some of the broccoli and chickpea mixture. Drizzle with olive oil and a sprinkle of red pepper flakes, if desired. If you're making appetizers, minimize the amount of olive oil you include, but if people have the option of using a knife and fork, you can be more generous with the drizzle.

NOTE: Consider saving the chickpea liquid, also known as aquafaba. You can use it in recipes like brownies and mayonnaise, found on pages 9 and 11.

Carrot tops are some of the prettiest produce scraps, and those bushy feathery greens are tasty, too. They have a fresh, earthy, and mildly bitter flavor (they are not poisonous, despite the persistent rumors suggesting so). If, like me, you enjoy bitter things, carrot tops can be consumed raw—try mixing some leaves in with milder greens in a salad (see page 48). If you'd rather tame their bitterness, blanch them first, and then use anywhere you would any other greens. I think carrot greens are especially great for punchy pesto (see page 52) and other green sauces, like gremolata, but if you really can't get behind the bitterness, add those fernlike fronds into a bouquet of flowers.

SHAVED ZUCCHINI SALAD WITH CARROT TOPS AND FENNEL SEED DUKKAH

FOR THE DUKKAH

2 tablespoons sesame seeds

1 tablespoon whole cumin seeds

2 teaspoons whole fennel seeds

1½ teaspoons coriander seeds

¼ cup shelled, roasted pistachio nuts

½ teaspoon freshly ground black pepper

½ teaspoon fine-grain sea salt

FOR THE SALAD

Greens from one medium-size bunch
    of carrots, plus 2 of the carrots
    (the carrots are optional)

2 medium-size zucchini or yellow
    squash

¼ teaspoon fine-grain sea salt

Extra virgin olive oil

Half a medium-size lemon

The ingredient *dukkah* is an Egyptian nut-and-spice blend; mine isn't all that traditional because it includes fennel seeds, but I happen to love the way the fennel seeds complement the bitter carrot greens.

If you have extra dukkah left over, it's a handy condiment to have around for sprinkling on other salads, hard-boiled eggs, or—as it is traditionally served—for an easy appetizer with crusty bread and olive oil (dip the bread in olive oil first and then in the dukkah). **SERVES 4**

1. In a medium-size saucepan, toast the sesame seeds, cumin seeds, fennel seeds, and coriander seeds over medium heat until the sesame seeds are lightly browned and the mixture smells fragrant, 2 to 3 minutes. Let cool slightly in the pan.

2. Place the seed mixture in a mortar with a pestle and crush to break down the seeds, then add the pistachios and gently pound until the nut pieces become peppercorn-size or smaller. Mix in the pepper and salt and set the dukkah aside.

3. Trim off the bottom stems of the carrot greens that have no leaves. (Save them for broth, page 129.)

4. Fill a medium-size pot with water and bring it to a boil over high heat.

5. Prepare an ice bath: Fill a medium-size bowl with ice and water.

6. Once the water is boiling, add the carrot greens to the pot—pushing down with tongs to make sure they all get in the water—and blanch for 1 minute.

7. Drain the greens into a colander and use the tongs to transfer the greens to the ice bath to stop the cooking process. Let the greens cool completely.

8. Squeeze any remaining water from the greens, roughly chop them, and set aside.

9. Cut the carrots, if using, and the zucchini lengthwise into thin ribbons using a sharp knife, vegetable peeler, mandoline (watch your fingers!), or a spiralizer.

10. Spread out the zucchini on a platter, sprinkle the carrot greens over the zucchini, then sprinkle with the carrot ribbons, if using, and the salt (you might not need a full ¼ teaspoon). Drizzle everything with olive oil and squeeze the lemon over the top. (I like to squeeze lemons over one cupped hand so I catch any seeds.) Generously sprinkle the dukkah over the top and serve family style.

CARROT TOP PESTO TARTLETS

Once your pesto is made, these little tartlets come together quickly—perfect for a last-minute appetizer that looks impressive, but doesn't take much effort. If you can find it, I like Dufour brand puff pastry—the ingredient list is short and recognizable, and it uses all butter (something that should be a given with puff pastry, but is not). **MAKES 16 SMALL APPETIZER-SIZE TARTS**

1 package (14 ounces) frozen puff pastry, defrosted in the refrigerator overnight (see headnote)

½ cup Carrot Top Pesto (page 52), about half a batch

16 to 24 grape tomatoes, sliced in half lengthwise

½ cup finely grated Grana Padano or other Parmesan-like cheese

Extra virgin olive oil, for drizzling

1. Preheat the oven to 350°F.

2. Spread out the puff pastry on a piece of parchment paper and gently use a rolling pin to flatten out any creases. Cut into 16 equal rectangles: First, cut the pastry into 4 pieces, then into 8, and then 16. (If you're using another brand of puff pastry, your tartlets might be square rather than rectangular—either way works!) Using a small, sharp knife, score a smaller rectangle about ¼ inch inside each of the 16 pieces. This might seem unnecessarily fussy, but it helps create and keep an edge on each of the tartlets.

3. Transfer the parchment paper with the puff pastry pieces to a baking sheet and nudge them away from each other a little bit so they aren't touching.

4. Spread each tartlet with ½ tablespoon of the pesto, staying within the boundaries of the scored inner rectangle. Place a few tomato halves on each tartlet, cut side up.

5. Bake until the pastry is fully cooked and the edges are golden brown, about 30 minutes.

6. Sprinkle the tartlets with Grana Padano, drizzle with a few drops of olive oil per tartlet, and serve.

CARROT TOP PESTO

Greens from 1 medium-size bunch of carrots (to make about 1 cup after blanching and chopping)
½ cup unsalted sunflower seeds, toasted (see page 22)
1 garlic clove, minced
1 tablespoon freshly squeezed lemon juice
¼ teaspoon fine-grain sea salt
¼ cup plus 1 tablespoon extra virgin olive oil

This makes a thick pesto, perfect for spreading on crackers or sandwiches or on puff-pastry tarts (see page 51). Alternatively, thin it out with more olive oil and use it as a dip for vegetables or as a sauce for pasta. I'm using the word "pesto" loosely here, as there's no cheese, but the carrot greens and sunflower seeds are so flavorful that you won't miss it.

If you can't find unsalted sunflower seeds, it's okay to use salted ones, just add the sea salt to taste (you most likely won't need it). **MAKES ABOUT 1 CUP**

1. Fill a medium-size pot with water and bring it to a boil over high heat.

2. Prepare an ice bath: Fill a medium-size bowl with ice and water.

3. Once the water is boiling, add the carrot greens to the pot— pushing down with tongs to make sure they all get in the water—and blanch for 1 minute.

4. Drain the pot into a colander and transfer the greens to the ice bath with the tongs to stop the cooking process. Let the greens cool completely and drain them.

5. Squeeze any remaining water from the greens and roughly chop them.

6. In a food processor, pulse the greens, sunflower seeds, garlic, lemon juice, and salt, scraping down the sides of the bowl as necessary. Then add the olive oil and process again until smooth.

While living in Japan, we were lucky enough to have numerous gracious hosts and countless good meals at their homes. This was an unusual treat, as it's more common there to entertain friends at a restaurant than at personal dwellings. One of our most memorable evenings included whisky tastings, grilled meats and seafood, and *nabemono* (basically "things cooked in a hot pot filled with broth"). There were a number of special dishes, but I was especially captivated by one of the appetizers—shiso leaves swimming in a spicy sesame-flavored broth. I'd never had anything like it. We all took turns plucking out individual leaves with chopsticks, and the combination of shiso's assertive bite with the spicy flavoring had me hooked—I ~~asked~~ begged our host for the recipe.

Our host, Ida-san, copied and then painstakingly translated the original recipe for me. It results in a paste that gets spread on shiso leaves. (I guess our host didn't follow the recipe either?) Over the years, I've kept most of the same ingredients, but tweaked their ratios. Shiso is one of my favorite herbs, but it can be challenging to find; in this case carrot tops make a surprisingly good substitute (in other situations you can substitute basil). As for the peppers, use whatever works for you heat-wise. I generally use one or two serranos or jalapeños, but if you'd like to tone down the heat, use a mini bell pepper—it won't add a lot of flavor, but it will add a nice pop of color to the dish. You can find *shichimi togarashi* (seven-spice powder) in Asian markets, spice shops, or online.

Kimchi is a Korean dish of salted and fermented vegetables; it often includes cabbage and radishes, though there are many different varieties of it. *Kimuchi* is the phonetic equivalent of kimchi in Japanese, and although similar, sometimes it's said to be less spicy. Unlike classic kimchi, it isn't always fermented, as is the case here. I've kept kimuchi in the name as homage to the original recipe, though it's stretching the definition—not only is it not fermented, there's also no cabbage. **SERVES 2 AS AN APPETIZER, OR 3 OR 4 AS A SIDE DISH**

SPICY CARROT TOP KIMUCHI

Greens from 1 medium-size bunch of carrots

1 tablespoon mirin (see Note, page 54)

1 garlic clove, minced

2 tablespoons toasted sesame seeds (see page 22 for more on toasting), ground (using either a spice grinder or mortar and pestle)

3 tablespoons soy sauce

1 tablespoon toasted sesame oil

Generous pinch of shichimi togarashi or smoked paprika

Thinly sliced peppers, to taste (see headnote)

1. Trim off the bottom stems of the carrot greens. They can be discarded or saved for broth (page 129).

2. Place the mirin, garlic, and ¼ cup water in a small saucepan and bring to a boil. Boil just long enough to take the edge off the garlic, less than a minute.

3. Remove the pan from the heat and mix in the sesame seeds, soy sauce, sesame oil, shichimi togarashi, and sliced peppers. Let it cool.

4. Place the carrot greens in a container and add the cooled soy sauce mixture. Cover and refrigerate, for at least 1 hour, preferably overnight. If you think about it, shake the container a few times. It will keep for 3 to 5 days.

5. To serve, grab chopsticks, pluck out a leaf, and enjoy. Or if that sounds too strange for an appetizer, chop the greens and eat them with a bowl of rice, or put them on sandwiches— I like them on cream cheese toast.

NOTE: You can find mirin in the international aisle of your grocery store, or at an Asian market, or online. This recipe calls for a small amount, so if you can't find it, either omit it entirely or substitute 1 tablespoon white wine and ¼ teaspoon granulated sugar.

If there's a ranking of underutilized, unappreciated produce parts, cauliflower cores and leaves are surely in the top five. The cores and little stem pieces that remain after cutting off the coveted florets can be used just as you would the florets: Thinly shave them, roast them, or, as in the case of the following recipe, cook them until soft and blend them into something else.

Cauliflower leaves are perfectly edible, too—they can be used just like any of your other favorite dark leafy greens. I suspect we often pull off the leaves and discard them without another thought, because unless you're growing your own cauliflower, there aren't all that many leaves to work with. Although you may not have enough to compose a dish of leaves alone, in many cases you can just add them along with the cauliflower flesh to the dish you're already making.

WHITE BEAN AND CAULIFLOWER CORE PUREE WITH GREEN OLIVE GREMOLATA

FOR THE PUREE

Core and any smaller stem pieces from
    1 large head cauliflower, chopped
    into a few large pieces

1 can (15 ounces) Great Northern beans
    (or similar white bean), drained, with
    liquid reserved

1 small garlic clove, minced

1 tablespoon freshly squeezed
    lemon juice

½ teaspoon fine-grain sea salt

FOR THE GREMOLATA

½ cup finely chopped fresh flat-leaf
    parsley

1 tablespoon lemon zest

1 medium-size garlic clove, grated with
    a Microplane or very finely minced

¼ cup chopped green olives

Extra virgin olive oil, for serving (optional)

I like this puree served as a dip—ideally at room temperature, but I've eaten it cold, too, straight out of the refrigerator—with pita or sturdy crackers. But you could also warm the puree, use it as a base for a piece of chicken or fish, and then top it all off with the gremolata.

Any variety of green olives will work—fancy ones from the grocery store olive bar or pimiento-stuffed ones from a jar—just be sure to pit them, if necessary, before chopping. **MAKES ABOUT 2 CUPS**

1. To make the puree: Fill a small or medium-size saucepan with water and bring to a boil over high heat, and add the cauliflower pieces. Return the water to a boil and cook until tender, 10 to 15 minutes, depending on the size of the pieces. Drain the cauliflower and let cool slightly.

2. In a food processor, blend together the cauliflower, beans, 1 tablespoon of the bean liquid, the garlic, lemon juice, and salt until smooth. If needed, add a bit more bean liquid to blend. Taste and adjust the seasoning as necessary. If you're going to be serving this as a dip, transfer it to a serving bowl.

3. To make the gremolata: Combine the parsley, lemon zest, garlic, and olives in a small bowl. Scatter the mixture across the top of the dip, drizzle with olive oil, if using, and serve. The puree can be made a couple of days ahead of time and the gremolata can be made 6 hours ahead of time. Once the two are layered on top of each other, the dip is at its best within a day or so.

If you have leftover bean liquid, keep it to make brownies (page 9) or aquafaba mayonnaise (page 11).

CLEAN out the **CRISPER**

Quick Pickles.

Making a batch of quick pickles is a good way not only to use up any scraps and stragglers in the produce bin of your refrigerator, but also to revive the ones that are starting to go limp (I'm looking at you, carrots and celery).

Kosher salt (or pickling salt) is ideal, because it won't make your brine cloudy like table salt can. Some cooks advise against using sea salt due to the trace minerals in it. I've never had an issue using sea salt in quick pickles, but I stick with kosher when I have it. Although any type of vinegar will work, I always use a light-colored variety, so the color of the pickle isn't impacted. Good options include apple cider vinegar, white wine or champagne vinegar, or rice vinegar. White distilled vinegar will work as well, but it does have a harsher flavor.

What should you pickle? Almost anything that sounds good to you. Green beans, asparagus, eggplant, peppers, peas, beets, carrots, radishes, cucumbers, celery —you get the idea. And don't stop at vegetables, try fruits as well such as grapes, apple slices, berries, and of course scraps—like the white part of watermelon rinds, cucumber ends and peels, and chard stalks.

I tend to use wide-mouth jars (it's easier to get the items back

out), mainly the pint or pint-and-a-half glass canning jars. I like to start with small batches, one or two jars at a time for multiple reasons: I like variety and don't want too much of any one pickle; it's easier to motivate yourself if you're not staring down a countertop full of jars; and, especially when you're pickling scraps, there probably isn't all that much of any one thing to pickle anyway.

I don't have a standard rule for how much brine to make for how many jars, because it will vary depending on what I'm putting in them (for instance, there will be more gaps around unripe cherry tomatoes than there will be for sliced kale stems)—I just make an educated guess. If you don't have quite enough to cover your pickles, add a bit more water; it will be fine. If that imprecision bugs you, Fred R. once shared a clever tip on Food52: Pack your jars with the items to be pickled, fill the jars with water, then empty the water into a measuring cup—that's how much brine you'll need.

TANGY FRIDGE PICKLES

Items to be pickled
   (see headnote for quantity)

Spices and/or herbs
   (optional—see Step 1)

Vinegar (see headnote)

Kosher salt (or pickling salt)

Granulated sugar
   (optional—see Step 3)

1. Pack your jars. Place your items to be pickled in a jar (or similar glass container) that has a lid or cover and add flavor with herbs and spices and other aromatics, things like mustard seeds, red pepper flakes, a crushed garlic clove, a knob of fresh ginger, citrus zest, fresh dill. Think about what you'd like your final result to be and play around with different combinations.

2. Make the brine. There's no hard and fast rule with quick pickle ingredient ratios, but just like I prefer my vinaigrette on the tangy side, so too do I like my pickles. I use a 3:1 ratio of vinegar to water and add 1 tablespoon salt for every (total) cup of liquid. There's your basic brine. If you'd prefer a pickle with less of a bite, use a 2:1 ratio of vinegar to water and add sugar—I generally don't add much, if any, but if you'd like to, you can add up to as much sugar as water.

3. I often just shake the brine in a jar to dissolve the salt, but you can also heat the brine in a pot on the stove to save time—go with this option if you're using more than a tablespoon or two of sugar.

4. Pour in the brine. Cover and refrigerate the brine-covered item for at least an hour or two, ideally longer to let it really pickle. They'll keep this way for a few weeks.

You don't always need to make a big production of pickling! If you ever have a small amount of something, like extra chopped shallots or onions, simply place them in a jar, add a pinch of sugar and a pinch of salt, cover with vinegar, and toss them in the fridge. They're a handy condiment to have on hand to liven up anything from salads and sandwiches to rice bowls and more.

Truth time: Celery hearts and leaves really don't deserve their reputation as scraps, for multiple reasons. Celery leaves make a garnish that's both pretty *and* tasty (I'm looking at you, flavorless Karma orchids and dried-out curly parsley sprigs). Both the leaves and the tender hearts are bursting with celery flavor, without any stringiness or intense crunchiness (nothing against celery's crunch—there are just times when it isn't as welcome). And both are incredibly versatile, seamlessly melding into everything from sauces and salads to spreads and breads.

Aioli may sound fancy, but it couldn't be easier to make yourself. After Food52 community member Pat K. used radish leaves in her aioli, I realized I wasn't playing around with my aioli enough; it's a blank slate for using all sorts of scraps (and non-scraps!). Note that although aioli usually can come together with a vigorous whisking session, this is not one of those recipes: You really need to use a mini food processor or an immersion blender to completely incorporate the celery leaves.

The celery leaf flavor is fairly mild, so I like it best as a dip for crudités or potato chips. You could also mix the aioli into egg, potato, or chicken salad or spread it on sandwiches—if you're worried the delicate flavor might be overwhelmed, use more celery leaves! Even if most of the leaves are lopped off the top of your celery heads, I find a lot of leaves hiding among the innermost small stalks, so make sure to include those. If you have trouble getting a cupful, it's easy to halve the recipe. **MAKES ABOUT 1 (GENEROUS) CUP**

CELERY LEAF AIOLI

2 large egg yolks (see Note)

1 cup celery leaves, unpacked, chopped

2 medium-size garlic cloves, minced

2 teaspoons freshly squeezed lemon juice

½ teaspoon fine-grain sea salt

¾ cup grapeseed or canola oil

¼ cup extra virgin olive oil

1. Process the egg yolks, celery leaves, garlic, lemon juice, and sea salt in a mini food processor until well blended.

2. While still processing, slowly drip the grapeseed oil one drop at a time through one of the small holes on the top of the food processor—this is essential for getting the aioli to emulsify, so don't rush it! Once about ¼ cup has been blended in, the aioli should be starting to thicken up. The remainder of the grapeseed oil can be added in a thin steady stream, still through the tiny hole on the top, while the machine is running. Then add the olive oil through the top, again in a slow, steady stream.

3. Store the aioli in an airtight container in the refrigerator for up to 3 days.

NOTE: Raw eggs aren't recommended for pregnant women, the very young, the very old, or anyone with a compromised immune system. If you're squeamish, stick with pasteurized eggs.

EGG SALAD SANDWICHES WITH CELERY HEARTS AND LEAVES

6 large eggs

½ teaspoon Dijon mustard

2 to 3 tablespoons mayonnaise

Fine-grain sea salt

Freshly ground black pepper

Innermost ribs of celery, leaves included, finely chopped (about ⅓ cup)

2 to 3 tablespoons finely chopped fresh dill or chives

4 or 8 slices of bread (depending on whether you want open-faced or traditional sandwiches)

4 to 8 leaves butter lettuce

The smallest yellow ribs at the very heart of a head of celery get very little love. They're not only tiny, but they're also so much more flexible than the outer ribs—not exactly a trait we typically look for in celery. But this makes them perfect for egg salad: They have just enough crunch to add textural variety, without being so crunchy as to take away from the comforting softness of the egg. If you want to go all-in on celery flavor, use Celery Leaf Aioli (page 61) in place of the mayonnaise.

Two suggestions: Use the best eggs you can buy, but fresher isn't better in this case—older eggs are actually easier to peel (see box). And these are simple sandwiches—try to resist the urge to pile on extra ingredients (unless it's avocado—in which case, proceed) lest you cover up the delicate flavor of both the eggs and celery. **MAKES 4 TRADITIONAL OR 8 OPEN-FACED SANDWICHES**

1. Place the eggs in a small pot and add enough cold water to cover by about an inch. Place the pot over high heat, and bring the water just to a boil. Turn off the heat and cover the pot. Let the eggs sit for 8 minutes, then remove them with a slotted spoon and run cold water over them until they are cool to the touch. This method will cook the eggs so that the yolks are fully set, yet still soft.

2. Peel the eggs, cut each one in half, set aside the whites, and place just the yolks in a medium-size bowl. Use a fork to mash the yolks together with the mustard, 2 tablespoons of the mayonnaise, a pinch of fine-grain sea salt, and a few grinds of pepper. If the mixture seems really thick, add the final tablespoon of mayonnaise.

3. Roughly chop the hard-boiled egg whites and add them to the bowl, along with the chopped celery and dill, and gently mix everything together.

4. Divide among 4 slices of bread and top each sandwich with a couple of lettuce leaves. If you're serving the sandwiches closed, top the lettuce with the remaining slices of bread.

How old is old? According to the American Egg Board, raw eggs in their shell are good for 4 to 5 weeks beyond the pack date or about 3 weeks after purchase. Freshly laid eggs are more likely to stick to the shell after hard cooking, so if you're buying them directly from a farmer, ideally wait a week or two before using them for egg salad. If you're buying eggs from the store, look for ones with the closest expiration date.

CHARD

I'm always seduced by the Swiss chard bundles with a mix of colored stalks. Nothing against white-stalked chard, but given the choice, I go rainbow all the way. It's almost like buying a bouquet of flowers; I'm mainly doing it for the joy the pop of colors brings me. Of course I'm not just looking at them—since I hate to waste food, I eat the stalks, too. And there are a multitude of options for them beyond merely chopped and sautéed along with the leaves: They can be pickled, braised, grilled, or gratinéed. Blanch or steam them and blend them into creamy dips or pesto (note that if you, too, use rainbow chard, these spreads will take on interesting hues).

ROASTED SWISS CHARD STEMS WITH A CREAMY SESAME DRESSING

2 tablespoons sesame seeds, toasted
(see page 22); plus more for garnish
(optional)

2 teaspoons rice vinegar

½ teaspoon mirin

½ teaspoon toasted sesame oil

1½ teaspoons soy sauce

2 tablespoons mayonnaise

1½ teaspoons Greek yogurt

Stems from 1 large bunch Swiss chard

Extra virgin olive oil

Freshly ground black pepper

My introduction to eating chard stems was through my colleague Kristen Miglore's Genius Recipe column on Food52. She shared chef and restauranteur Anna Klinger's recipe for Grilled Swiss Chard Stems with Anchovy Vinaigrette, and I was besotted with the idea of a recipe centered around a produce part that you're typically instructed to remove and discard. I loved the idea of eating chard stems cloaked in sauce but wanted to streamline the prep, opting to forgo Anna's blanching and grilling in favor of just roasting and drizzling with an Asian-inspired dressing. Any leftover dressing can be stored separately in the fridge for 3 to 5 days. **MAKES A SIDE DISH FOR 2 TO 4**

1. Preheat the oven to 425°F.

2. Crush the toasted sesame seeds with a spice grinder or a mortar and pestle.

3. In a small bowl, whisk together the sesame seeds, rice vinegar, mirin, sesame oil, soy sauce, mayonnaise, and yogurt and set aside.

4. Cut the chard stems into 5- to 6-inch lengths, place them on a baking sheet, and drizzle them with a little olive oil. Gently toss them together to get the stems evenly coated. Spread out into a single layer and lightly sprinkle with pepper.

5. Roast the stems until the centers are tender when pierced with a knife, the edges are starting to char, and any lingering leaf pieces crisp up like kale chips, 7 to 10 minutes.

6. Divide the roasted stems among plates, drizzle with the sesame dressing, and sprinkle with the remaining toasted sesame seeds, if using. Serve hot.

I think everyone has a crisis ingredient: It's that
one thing you still have in your fridge, even if it's mostly bare.
A crisis ingredient can limp along and help you pull a meal
together. But if you're out of that one thing, there is suddenly
no food in the house! You have to go grocery shopping! That
food for me is cheese. I always have multiple kinds of cheese
on hand at all times and I keep multiple zip-top bags going in
the freezer at all times, too, for extra bits and rinds. One for
Parmesan rinds (for broth, page 129), one for blue cheese, one
for Cheddar, and one for a mix of all sorts of cheeses: goat,
Gouda, Brie, Asiago, Jack, Colby, Manchego—any kind (these
bags will come in handy for the three cheese spreads ahead,
pages 68, 70, 71). Please remember to use common sense
when saving rinds: Don't save (or eat) wax, wood, or any other
nonedible wrappings!

CHEESE RIND
FROMAGE FORT

1 pound leftover cheese bits and rinds,
    keeping rinds to no more than
    two thirds of the total

1 garlic clove, minced

⅓ cup dry white wine

1 to 2 tablespoons unsalted butter,
    room temperature

Softened butter or cream cheese,
    for serving (optional)

Finely chopped fresh herbs, such as
    chives, dill, and parsley, and
    flaky sea salt, for garnish (optional)

Lightly toasted baguette slices or
    crackers, for serving

Even if you're familiar with *fromage fort*, the French cheese spread that literally means "strong cheese" (the combination of cheese, wine, and garlic can pack a punch!), you've probably been making it with leftover nubs of cheese—but you should be using the rinds, too!

You can use any mix of cheese bits and rinds you like for this recipe, but keep in mind that if you use any blue cheese in this blend, it doesn't take much for it to taste like a blue cheese dip. You can dress this up with freshly ground black pepper, a pinch or two of cayenne pepper, or a couple of tablespoons of minced fresh herbs like chives or parsley. All varieties should be served at room temperature—with lightly toasted baguette slices or sturdy crackers. **MAKES A GENEROUS 2 CUPS**

1. Chop any large pieces of cheese into smaller, bite-size pieces and grate any hard cheeses—very hard rinds are best grated in the food processor with the grating disk.

2. If you used the grating disk, take it out, remove the cheese from the food processor, and swap in the chopping blade. Add the cheese and garlic to the food processor and process.

3. Add the wine and 1 tablespoon butter and process again until it comes together as a thick spread. If it doesn't seem like it's quite coming together, add the additional tablespoon butter and process again.

4. Transfer the Fromage Fort to an airtight container or zip-top bag and chill to let the flavors meld; it will keep in the refrigerator for up to 5 days and in the freezer for up to 3 months—please note that the flavors will intensify the longer it chills.

5. When ready to serve, remove the Fromage Fort from the refrigerator or freezer and allow it to come to room temperature. If you used a large percentage of rinds, you'll find that the mixture becomes more crumbly in the refrigerator. If it doesn't fully come back together, stir in a bit of softened butter or cream cheese until it reaches the desired consistency.

6. Transfer the cheese to a board, sprinkle with the herbs and sea salt, if using, and serve with the baguette slices.

Make a decadent open-faced cheese sandwich: Spread Cheese Rind Fromage Fort on a lightly toasted piece of bread and then put it in the broiler until it's warm and toasty.

CHEDDAR NUB PUB CHEESE

1 pound leftover Cheddar bits
    and rinds (rinds no more than
    two thirds of the total)

1 teaspoon prepared horseradish

½ teaspoon Worcestershire sauce

2 teaspoons Dijon mustard

½ cup brown beer or pale ale

1 to 2 tablespoons cream cheese

Softened butter or cream cheese,
    for serving (optional)

This spread has a mild but well-balanced flavor; if you'd like more of a kick, add a little more horseradish or a few dashes of hot sauce. Aside from baguette rounds and sandwiches, this spread is a perfect match as a dip for sturdy pretzels or a spread for soft pretzels. **MAKES A GENEROUS 2 CUPS**

1. Chop any large pieces of cheese into smaller, bite-size pieces and grate any hard cheeses—very hard rinds are best grated in the food processor with the grating disk.

2. If you used the grating disk, take it out, remove the cheese from the food processor, and swap in the chopping blade. Add the cheese, horseradish, Worcestershire sauce, and mustard to the food processor and process until combined.

3. Add the beer and 1 tablespoon cream cheese and process again until it comes together as a thick spread. If it doesn't seem like it's quite coming together, add the remaining tablespoon cream cheese and process again.

4. Transfer the pub cheese to an airtight container or zip-top bag and chill to let the flavors meld; it will keep in the refrigerator for up to 5 days and in the freezer for up to 3 months—please note that the flavors will intensify the longer it chills.

5. When ready to serve, remove the pub cheese from the freezer or refrigerator and allow it to come to room temperature. If you used a large percentage of rinds, you'll find that the mixture becomes more crumbly in the refrigerator. If it doesn't fully come back together, stir in a little softened butter or cream cheese until it reaches the desired consistency.

As with the basic Cheese Rind Fromage Fort (page 68), you can dress this up with freshly ground pepper, a pinch or two of cayenne pepper in place of the hot sauce, or a couple of tablespoons of minced fresh herbs like chives or parsley. **MAKES A GENEROUS 2 CUPS**

1. Chop any large pieces of cheese into smaller, bite-size pieces and grate any hard cheeses—very hard rinds are best grated in the food processor with the grating disk.

2. If you used the grating disk, take it out, remove the cheese from the food processor, and swap in the chopping blade. Add the cheese, garlic, brandy, and 3 tablespoons cream cheese to the food processor and process until the mixture comes together as a thick spread. If you used a lot of crumbly rather than creamy blue cheese, it might not look like it's quite coming together—add an additional tablespoon cream cheese and process again. Taste and add a few dashes of hot sauce, if desired, then process again.

3. The spread is likely to be an interesting shade of gray or beige, so I like to spread it into a serving bowl, sprinkle the pecans in a layer across the top for serving (though if you'd rather, they could also be mixed in), and then drizzle the honey over everything.

4. Transfer the Blue Cheese Spread (without the pecans or honey) to an airtight container or zip-top bag, and chill to let the flavors meld; it will keep in the refrigerator for up to 5 days and in the freezer for up to 3 months—please note that the flavors will intensify the longer it chills.

5. When ready to serve, remove the cheese spread from the freezer or refrigerator and allow it to come to room temperature. If you used a large percentage of rinds, you'll find that the mixture becomes more crumbly in the refrigerator. If it doesn't fully come back together, add a little more softened cream cheese.

BLUE CHEESE SPREAD WITH PECANS

1 pound leftover cheese bits and rinds (at least half of the mix blue cheese, rinds no more than two thirds of the total)

1 garlic clove, minced

2 tablespoons brandy

3 tablespoons cream cheese, plus more as needed

Hot sauce (optional; I tend to go with a vinegary one for this, like Frank's RedHot)

1/3 to 1/2 cup toasted chopped pecans (see page 22)

1 to 2 tablespoons honey

These brothy beans are inspired by a recipe that Food52 cofounder Merrill Stubbs makes—they're a stripped-down, vegetarian take on hers. The shorter ingredient list is offset by a couple of slightly fussy steps, but that—along with really good dried beans—is what keeps this dish from being basic, boring beans. Serve them as is, or make them a meal by topping them with a poached egg and some greens—or a scoop of Charred Asparagus End Pesto (page 21). **SERVES 6 TO 8 AS A SIDE DISH**

1. Place the beans in a large pot and add 8 cups water.

2. Preheat the oven to 375°F. Slice each head of garlic in half horizontally, and discard most of the papery outer covering (you want the heads to remain intact). Put the heads back together, set each one on a small piece of aluminum foil, and drizzle with olive oil. Wrap the aluminum foil up around each head to seal it into a packet. Bake until the garlic cloves are soft, about 40 minutes. Set aside to cool. Turn off the oven.

3. The beans will have expanded after soaking, so make sure they're still covered by the soaking water, but not by very much. Add the onion halves, Parmesan rind, and thyme to the pot and bring to a boil over medium-high heat; keep at a boil for 10 minutes. Then partially cover the pot and reduce the heat to keep the beans at a gentle simmer—medium or medium-low heat, depending on your stovetop. If the water level drops below the beans, add hot water from a teakettle to just barely cover them again—don't add too much!

4. Cook until tender—as little as 40 minutes or as much as 3 hours. It's important to go by taste, because bean freshness, size, and soaking can affect cooking time. Once the beans are tender, remove and discard the Parmesan rind and thyme stems. Remove the onion halves and place them in a tall narrow container. Squeeze in the garlic cloves from one of the roasted heads, and puree using an immersion blender. (A mini food processor would also work.)

5. Add the garlic and onion puree to the pot of beans along with the salt and vinegar. Taste and adjust seasonings as necessary. Ladle the beans into bowls and garnish each with black pepper, grated Parmesan, and a scoop of pesto, if desired. Serve with bread smeared with the remaining roasted garlic.

BROTHY BEANS WITH ROASTED GARLIC AND PARMESAN RIND

1 pound dry white beans, soaked (I try to soak them for 2 to 4 hours—it will speed up their cooking time and help them cook more evenly. Soaking isn't essential if the timing doesn't work with your schedule; they'll just take longer to cook in Step 4.)

2 heads garlic

Extra virgin olive oil

1 medium-size white onion, peeled, halved, and root end just barely trimmed so the layers remain together

1 Parmesan rind

3 sprigs thyme

2½ teaspoons fine-grain sea salt

1 teaspoon apple cider vinegar or white wine vinegar

Freshly ground black pepper, for serving

Freshly grated Parmesan cheese, for garnish (optional)

Charred Asparagus End Pesto (page 21), for garnish (optional)

Slices of crusty bread, for serving (optional)

As a warm-weather lover who lives in Michigan, I think of citrus fruits as sweet little personal sanity saviors in the dead of winter. Whether you're still trying to unbury yourself from two feet of snow or are just trying to come to terms with the umpteenth gray day in a row, citrus fruits are here for you. The dreariness outside is abated—at least a little bit—by their vibrant flavors and cheery colors, reminders that eating seasonally in the wintertime needn't be restricted to greens and storage crops. And it's not just their juice and flesh that should be brightening up your dishes—the rinds should be put to good use, too!

VANILLA POD– SCENTED CANDIED LEMON PEELS

4 or 5 lemons (It's fine to use spent
    lemons; it just might be more
    challenging to separate the fruit
    from the peel.)
1 spent vanilla pod (already split in half,
    seeds used elsewhere)
2 cups vanilla pod sugar (page 165) or
    granulated sugar

Candied citrus peels are popular around the holidays, but they don't need to be relegated to a single time of year! Make them anytime you know you'll be using a lot of citrus fruits. I'm using lemons here, but feel free to sub in other types of citrus rinds, as shown in the photo. Plan ahead! You won't be eating these the day you make them; they need to dry overnight. Added bonus: The candying syrup can be saved for stirring into tea or a hot toddy (page 164). **MAKES A GENEROUS 2 CUPS**

1. Cut each lemon into quarters, and, using your fingers to get under the flesh, separate the fruit from the peel, working to keep as much pith attached to the peel as possible. It's okay if a little fruit remains stuck to the peel at this point. (Use the flesh of the lemons elsewhere or juice them and save for another use.)

2. Place the peels in a medium-size saucepan, add cold water until the pan is nearly full, and bring to a full boil over medium-high or high heat. Boil the peels for 2 minutes, then drain the water and repeat this step two more times, with fresh cold water each time. This is essential for removing excess bitterness, and it also tenderizes the peels.

3. Let the peels cool to the touch. If desired, cut the peels into strips. Either way, if any lingering fruit remains stuck to the peels, gently scrape it off. Set aside.

4. Combine the vanilla pod, 1½ cups of the sugar, and 1½ cups water in a medium-size saucepan over medium-high heat. Gently stir occasionally to help the sugar dissolve. Once the sugar has dissolved, add the peels and turn the heat down to medium-low. Simmer the peels until they become translucent, then simmer a couple of minutes more. This will take anywhere from 60 to 90 minutes. Resist the urge to stir, just gently nudge down the peels on the top every 15 minutes or so. Adjust the heat as necessary throughout the process to keep them at a gentle simmer. If you have a candy thermometer, the temperature should be around 230°F.

5. Set a cooling rack on a baking sheet (lined with parchment paper, if you have it, for easier cleanup) to catch drips. Using tongs or a slotted spoon, transfer a few candied peels at a time

to the cooling rack, letting excess liquid drip back into the pot before transferring. Discard the vanilla pod.

6. Make sure the peels are spread out in one layer on the rack, touching as little as possible. Let them dry overnight, uncovered.

7. When the peels are dry, add the remaining ½ cup sugar to a small bowl and toss a handful of peels at a time in the sugar to coat them. (If you're using the more precious vanilla sugar, you might want to start with ¼ cup and add more as needed, so you're sure not to waste any.)

8. Store in an airtight container, with some of the remaining sugar in the bottom, in a cool, dry place for up to 2 months. Alternatively, freeze in a single layer, then transfer to an airtight container and freeze for up to 6 months.

SHORTBREAD WITH HONEY-GLAZED GRAPEFRUIT PEEL AND PINK PEPPERCORNS

Every holiday season my maternal grandmother (Nana to me) would make who-knows-how-many dozens of cookies to give as gifts and enjoy with family and friends. She stored them all in tins, stacked precariously high on top of the extra refrigerator in the garage. After a meal, one of us grandkids would step out to get them, feet chilled by the concrete floor as we hurried back inside with our precious cargo. The two kinds I remember most are her toffee bars, though as a child I never understood why you would ruin a perfectly good cookie with nuts (in truth, I still have my doubts about the practice), and shortbread, a four-ingredient, couldn't-be-easier cookie that my chocolate-loving self should have eschewed, but I loved for its simple goodness. I've loosely adapted her base recipe, still keeping it pretty simple, but adding a little bit of a bite from grapefruit peel and pink peppercorns—I hope she would have approved.

You'll notice that this recipe calls for the peel from only a half grapefruit, so a full grapefruit lends enough peel for two batches. But don't be tempted to double the recipe. This is a dry dough that will become too hard to work with if you double it. By all means, make two batches, just make them separately. **MAKES 8 TO 16 COOKIES**

1. If you haven't yet peeled your grapefruit and are starting with a whole one, score the peel into quarters. Use your fingers to get under the flesh and separate the fruit from the peel, working to keep as much pith attached to the peel as possible. You can use the same method with half a grapefruit and fewer score marks. (Use the flesh of the grapefruit elsewhere or juice it and save for another use.)

2. Slice two of the quarters of peel into thin strips, and then cut those crosswise, so you end up with fine dice. Place the diced peel in a small saucepan over medium to medium-low heat along with the honey and 1 tablespoon of the sugar, and cook until the peel starts to appear translucent, about 5 minutes. (It won't become as translucent as, say, sautéed onions, but it will start to take on a stained-glass appearance.) Set aside and let cool slightly.

3. Preheat the oven to 300°F.

4. Cream together the butter and the remaining 4 tablespoons sugar in a medium-size bowl with a wooden spoon until smooth. (You could also use a hand or stand mixer, but for some reason I never want to dirty them for a small batch of cookies.)

5. Whisk together the flour, cornstarch, and ground peppercorns in a small bowl.

6. Add the flour mixture to the butter mixture and combine, first stirring with the wooden spoon, and then using your hands. Once it's all well combined, mix in the honey-glazed grapefruit peel. The dough will look very dry, less like dough and more like crumbles, but it should clump together when you squeeze some in your hand. If it isn't clumping, drizzle in up to 1 tablespoon water, and mix again.

7. Dump the crumbly dough onto a parchment- or silicone mat–lined baking sheet, and use your hands to press it together and form it into any shape you wish, between ⅓ and ½ inch thick. Then use a fork to score the dough so it can be easily cut after baking. My grandmother always made hers round and scored it into 8 wedges. I've taken to making a long rectangular shape and scoring 12 to 16 smaller rectangles.

8. Bake until golden brown around the edges, 20 to 25 minutes. Let cool and store in an airtight container for up to 1 week.

Peel from ½ grapefruit
(It's fine to use a spent half; it just might be more challenging to separate the fruit from the peel.)
2 tablespoons honey
5 tablespoons granulated sugar
½ cup unsalted butter, softened
1½ cups all-purpose flour
2 teaspoons cornstarch
1 generous teaspoon pink peppercorns, coarsely ground

Spent coffee grounds still hold *a lot* of flavor, more than enough to lend their roasty goodness to dishes savory and sweet. They can be put to use everywhere from rubs for meat to sweet treats like cakes and ice cream. For any recipes that call for ground coffee, you can swap in spent grounds instead. (Note that you probably wouldn't want to swap grounds in for instant espresso powder, since in many cases espresso powder would dissolve or be undetectable texture-wise, which is not the case with coffee grounds!) While the grind size won't matter in most cases, the quality of the coffee will: A high-quality coffee will lend a lot of flavor to the final recipe—older, less flavorful beans, not as much. Leftover brewed coffee can be put to use in a lot of ways too, like to amp up the flavor of chocolaty baked goods, and can be frozen for later use (in ice cube trays for easy portioning or to add to iced coffee).

During a visit to New York, I noticed one of my colleagues with a plateful of stuffed dates, which, I learned, were stuffed with a coffee-flavored peanut butter. That peanut butter came in a jar and had freshly ground coffee beans in it, but I figured that used coffee grounds would impart the same flavor. They did! So make yourself a pot of good coffee and save the grounds for nut butter. We use a French press in our home, so the beans are coarsely ground, but finely ground grounds are fine, too (say that five times fast).

Note that you'll need a large food processor for this one. The resulting cashew butter will be smooth, with a rich cocoa color and tiny flecks of grounds and nibs. If you'd prefer more texture, see the Variation that follows. Feel free to play around with different nuts and other additions, too. (Honey? Cocoa powder? Shredded coconut? Why not?) **MAKES ABOUT 2 CUPS**

1. Preheat the oven to 350° F.

2. Spread out the cashews on a rimmed baking sheet and toast them in the oven until lightly browned, 8 to 12 minutes. Let the nuts cool slightly.

3. Transfer the nuts to your food processor, add the salt, and pulse a few times, until the nuts start to look sandy.

4. Add the coffee grounds, cocoa nibs (if you're using them), and the oil, and process until smooth, scraping down the bowl of the food processor as needed. (This can take awhile, so be patient!)

5. Transfer to an airtight container and store in the refrigerator for 2 to 3 weeks. To serve, bring to room temperature.

COFFEE GROUND CASHEW BUTTER

2 cups raw cashews (whole or pieces)
½ teaspoon fine sea salt
2 tablespoons used coffee grounds
2 tablespoons cocoa nibs (optional)
¼ cup neutral-flavored oil, such as vegetable

In Step 4, add the oil to the cashews and process until smooth, then add the coffee grounds and cocoa nibs (if using), and pulse to combine. Scrape down the bowl of the food processor as needed. For even more texture, withhold a small handful of cashews and add them at the end along with the grounds and nibs.

VARIATION:
CRUNCHY COFFEE GROUND CASHEW BUTTER

CLEAN *out* **the** **CRISPER**

Salts.

I hadn't thought about how I could be using tomato skins until I read chef Gabrielle Hamilton's cookbook, *Prune*, in which she dries them and turns them into powder. While powders have their place in a restaurant, they aren't always easy to incorporate into everyday meals at home. Once the basic method is tweaked to make tomato skin salt ... well, now we're talking.

The result is the perfect summertime salt. The tomato flavor is definitely there (and yes, it does make fresh tomatoes taste even more tomato-y), but don't let that constrain you when you're thinking about how to use it. Sprinkle it over everything from eggs to corn on the cob. Use it to rim glasses for Bloody Marys. I'm certain you'll admire its pretty pinkish-red color any time you set out a little cellar of salt—like to accompany fresh radishes with butter.

Try this method with other types of scraps, too—like celery leaves, carrot peelings, citrus zests, or dried mushrooms (I can't be the only one who buys a package only to use part of it and then wonders what to do with the rest).

TOMATO SKIN SALT

SERVINGS WILL VARY WITH THE NUMBER OF TOMATOES USED

Tomato skins (see Notes)

Kosher salt (in equal amount to tomato skins by weight— see Notes)

1. Preheat the oven to 200°F.

2. After blanching and peeling tomatoes for some other use, save the tomato skins and weigh them (see Notes). Spread out the tomato skins on a parchment- or silicone mat–lined baking sheet so they don't overlap and sprinkle with the coarse salt that you've measured out to be equal in weight to the tomato skins.

3. Place the baking sheet in the oven and bake until the tomato skins are completely dry, like salt-encrusted autumn leaves. For the skins of 4 medium-size tomatoes, this takes 2 to 3 hours; larger batches will take longer.

4. Remove from the oven and let cool. Then use a spice mill or mortar and pestle to pulverize the salty skins into tomato skin salt. A small food processor works, too, but you might not be able to get the skins to break down as finely.

NOTES: Even if you generally don't mind tomato skins, bits of skin can be off-putting in sauces and soups, so recipes often call for peeled tomatoes. I think the easiest way to peel tomatoes is to fill a pot with water and bring to a boil over high heat. While you're waiting for it to boil, cut an ✕ in the bottom of each tomato and prepare an ice bath by filling a medium-size bowl with ice and water. Once the water is boiling, gently add the tomatoes (don't overcrowd them), and cook until the edges of the ✕ begin to peel back, 15 to 20 seconds. Transfer them to the ice bath, and once they're cool enough to handle, peel away the skin.

If you don't have a scale, don't worry about it—the recipe will work just fine. I've found the skins from 4 medium-size tomatoes generally amount to around 45 grams. And note that different salts have different densities. To get to 45 grams with Diamond Crystal Kosher Salt, use ¼ cup; with Morton Coarse Kosher Salt, use 3 tablespoons. Don't worry too much if you're not sure how much you should use of whatever salt you have, just go with your best guess—the salt blend will just be slightly more or less tomato-y.

yellow bell pepper
salt

tomato skins

celery
salt

tomato skin
salt

cucumber
salt

lime peel
salt

mushroom skin
salt

Sugars.

When Food52er Rhonda T. made her family's Third Generation Peaches, which calls for 5 cups of peeled and sliced peaches, she was left with a lot of peach peels. She set them aside, thinking she could dry them and grind them together with a little sugar, and then, serendipitously, she came across my recipe for Tomato Skin Salt (page 82), which gave her a guideline to follow.

Just as you can use the Tomato Skin Salt recipe (page 82) to make all sorts of flavored salts with scraps, so too can you follow this method to make all sorts of flavored sugars. I made a pear peel and cinnamon sugar combo here, but try it with peach peels as Rhonda did, or other fruit peels, like apple or plum.

Experiment with the type of sugar you use, too. I frequently use granulated sugar, and mix the resulting sugars into oatmeal, sprinkle them on top of Danish Pancakes with Apple Core Syrup (page 3), or use them in place of granulated sugar in baked goods, but a coarser sugar like turbinado would work as well, and could be used to sprinkle on top of pies or other baked goods.

tangerine peel
sugar

lemon peel
sugar

blood orange
peels

PEAR PEEL CINNAMON SUGAR

SERVINGS WILL VARY WITH THE NUMBER OF PEARS USED

Pear skins

Sugar (in equal amount to pear skins by weight, see Note)

Ground cinnamon

1. Preheat the oven to 200°F.

2. After peeling pears for some other use (poached pears, perhaps?), save the skins and weigh them (see Note). Spread out the pear peels on a parchment- or silicone mat–lined baking sheet so they aren't overlapping.

3. Place the baking sheet in the oven and bake until the peels are completely dry. For the peels of a small batch, like 4 medium-size pears, this takes 1 to 2 hours; larger batches will take longer.

4. Let the peels cool to the touch on the baking sheet, and then transfer them to a cooling rack to completely cool. (If you can stand to wait, let them hang out overnight to make sure they're completely dry.)

5. Grind the dry peels in a mini food processor or spice grinder and mix together with the sugar. Mix in cinnamon to taste.

NOTE: As a guideline, I've found the peels from 4 pears weigh around 80 grams, and after adding 80 grams of sugar (between ⅓ and ½ cup), I mix in about a teaspoon of ground cinnamon. If you don't have a scale, don't worry about it—the recipe will still work just fine. Proceed with the recipe through Step 4, then eyeball or measure the amount of ground peels and add in the same amount of sugar.

blood orange peel sugar

pear peel sugar

plum peel sugar

COLLARD GREENS

Kale gets a lot of eye-rolls lately. It's trendy enough to make it onto the menus of fast-food chains, and once any vegetable reaches that level of popularity, it has arguably jumped the shark, or at least, approached an oversaturation point. I, for one, love kale, and will never quit kale salads, but agree that it might be time to let a few other dark, leafy greens share space on our plates—starting with collard greens. Kale and collards are closely related—in fact, they share the same classification (*Brassica oleracea*, acephala group) and can be used in many of the same ways. My favorite comment on collard greens comes from blogger Tom Hirschfeld, who once said: "Sure, you could hang out with the pretty people and eat kale, but kale isn't collards. Neither are mustard or turnip greens. For me, because they are like the brainy girl who likes to read, collards are far more interesting." In that case, collard greens might just be my spirit vegetable.

W hile most of the recipes in the book are really built around a scrap, this is one of the few where the scrap cooks down until it basically disappears. In fact, it works just fine without the collard stems, and it would also work with the stems of other types of produce, like kale or chard.

When I'm eating pasta with a tomato-based sauce, I want it to be *really* saucy. Case in point: I think spaghetti should be served in a bowl, not on a plate. If you are not passionate about extra sauce or happen to like crispy edges of noodles in baked pasta dishes, use one 28-ounce and one 14-ounce can of crushed tomatoes instead of two big ones. The sauce is based on my favorite tomato-based one, Marcella Hazan's Tomato Sauce—the biggest difference being that she has you discard the onion after it has flavored the sauce, but I always like to blend it in. For a texture contrast, sometimes I like to add a crispy topping: Toss a cup of panko (Japanese breadcrumbs) with 2 to 3 tablespoons of melted butter and sprinkle on the top before baking.

Baked pasta dishes often call for cooking at a lower temperature for a long time, but I've come to prefer the technique employed by Al Forno, a restaurant in Providence, Rhode Island. They bake at 500°F for just 10 minutes, at such a high heat that you get bubbly cheese and a toasted top without having to wait around an unnecessarily long time for dinner. **SERVES 4 TO 6**

COLLARD STEM AND LEMONY RICOTTA STUFFED SHELLS

Salting the water really does make a difference in your pasta—it's the only chance you get to season the pasta itself. Don't be shy with the salt—you want the water to taste like the sea!

FOR THE FILLING

Stems from 1 bunch of collard greens
(see Note)

1 container (15 ounces) ricotta cheese

2/3 cup sliced black olives

1 heaping tablespoon lemon zest

1/4 teaspoon fine-grain sea salt

Freshly ground black pepper

FOR THE SAUCE

2 cans (28 ounces each) plain
crushed tomatoes

4 tablespoons unsalted butter

1 large white or yellow onion, cut into
eighths

FOR THE REST OF THE DISH

20 jumbo pasta shells (around half of a
12-ounce package)

Extra virgin olive oil

1 ball (4 ounces) fresh mozzarella,
torn into 1/2-inch pieces

1. Fill a medium-size pot with water and bring it to a boil over high heat. Cook the collard stems until they are very tender, 25 to 35 minutes. Drain, let them cool slightly, then roughly chop them.

2. Meanwhile, combine the crushed tomatoes, butter, and onion in another medium-size pot, and simmer while the stems cook for at least 20 minutes, ideally more like 45—feel free to let it continue simmering away until you're ready to use it. After it has cooked long enough for the onion to soften, use an immersion blender to puree the onion into the sauce and add a pinch or two of salt, to taste.

3. Place the collard stems in a mini food processor with about half of the ricotta (no need to measure—you just need something to help the stems blend) and process until very smooth. Add that mixture to a small bowl along with the rest of the ricotta, the black olives, and lemon zest and stir to combine. Add the salt and a few grinds of black pepper and mix again.

4. Fill another medium-size or large pot (or wash and reuse the collard stem pot) with salted water (see box, page 87) and bring it to a boil over high heat. Cook the pasta shells until al dente, according to the time suggested on the package. Take care not to overcook them, or they'll fall apart when you try to stuff them. Drain and toss with a teaspoon or two of olive oil to prevent them from sticking together.

5. Preheat the oven to 500°F.

6. Ladle about half of the sauce into the bottom of a 9-by-13-inch pan.

7. Fill each shell with a generous tablespoon of filling, and nestle them into the pan, open side up. Ladle the rest of the sauce over the shells, scatter the mozzarella over the top, and bake until the cheese is melted and the sauce is bubbling, about 10 minutes.

NOTE: If you don't have plans for the leaves of the collards, you can chiffonade them and then add them to the sauce before pureeing the onions in Step 2.

Your corn's husks and cobs are just as tasty as the kernels (okay, maybe not *just* as tasty, but very close), and can be put to use in a variety of ways. Add the cobs to flavor stock (see page 129), then use the stock for extra-corny soups or risotto or as a steaming liquid for seafood. Husks can be dried—either in the sun or on low heat in the oven—and used to wrap tamales, but I'm partial to toasting them in the oven and using them to infuse bourbon (see page 148).

While living in Japan, my husband and I took a mini getaway to an *onsen* (hot springs) resort in the mountains of Gifu prefecture. The scenery was incredible, but the food was what sold me on a return visit a few months later. Dinner seemed to last for hours, with small seasonal courses coming out in an endless stream. One of my favorite dishes was a rice ball that was mixed with a starchy, locally grown potato and grilled in a pan over a fire until it was perfectly crispy on every side.

Then, a few years after we'd moved back to the States, a pen pal friend in Japan, Kat N., blogged about making corn *yaki onigiri* (the name for these grilled rice balls), and I figured I could get the same corn flavor in a rice ball using just corn cobs. This version is "grilled" in a cast-iron pan—no open flames necessary. For the best results, you'll want to have a pastry brush on hand for applying soy sauce to the rice balls. If you don't have one, try pouring a small amount of soy sauce in a shallow dish and briefly dipping the top and bottom in (dipping every side would likely make it too salty, as the rice balls will soak up more soy sauce than you would have brushed on). And if you have a rice cooker, by all means, use it. **MAKES ABOUT 6 RICE BALLS**

1. Wash the rice in a bowl of water by swirling your fingers through it in a circular motion—the water will become cloudy (yes, even if the packaging says that washing or rinsing isn't necessary). Change the water a few times, continuing to swirl the rice with your fingers each time, until the water remains nearly clear. Drain the rice well and place it in a small heavy saucepan with 1 cup plus 2 tablespoons fresh cold water. If time allows, let the rice soak for 30 minutes to an hour.

2. Scrape down the sides of the corn cobs with a knife, and add the remnants of corn kernels and corn milk to the pot with the rice, and then add the cobs too, breaking them in half with your hands (or chopping them in half with a knife), if necessary, to fit.

3. Bring the water to a boil over medium-high heat, turn the heat down to low, and cover the pot. After about 12 minutes,

CORN COB YAKI ONIGIRI (GRILLED RICE BALLS)

1 cup medium- or short-grain white rice (sushi rice)

2 corn cobs, stripped of their kernels (see Note)

1 to 2 teaspoons unsalted butter

1 tablespoon soy sauce

Black and white sesame seeds, for garnish (optional)

remove the lid, stir the rice, and then re-cover the pot. Remove the pot from the heat and let stand, covered, for the rice to absorb the water fully, 10 to 15 minutes.

4. Transfer the rice to a large bowl to help it cool down faster, and discard the corn cobs—they've given you all they've got. Once the rice is cool enough to touch, wet both of your hands (so it doesn't stick to them), take a handful and begin forming it into a triangular shape (a stumpy three-dimensional triangle prism if you're being technical). Press firmly, but just until it holds its shape, not so firmly that it breaks apart. The triangular shape is the traditional one—it gives you a flat surface on every side for grilling—but if you find it too challenging, start with a round, burger-patty shape (in which case you'll just grill the top and the bottom) until you get the hang of it.

5. Grease the bottom of a cast-iron skillet, or a heavy, nonstick pan, with a small amount—about 1 teaspoon—of butter and place over medium heat. Once the pan is hot, add the onigiri. You can do this in two batches depending on the size of your pan and the number of onigiri. Let the onigiri get crispy and lightly browned on a side before turning them to a new side, about 5 minutes per side, adding more butter to the pan midway through the process if necessary. Don't move the onigiri unless you are shifting them to a new side, as they need to sit still to get their crispy crust.

6. Once you've crisped them on all sides, turn the heat down to low. (This is important! Burnt soy sauce doesn't taste good.) Lightly brush every side of every onigiri with soy sauce—you won't use the full amount. Pour a thin layer of sesame seeds, if using, onto a plate. Briefly recrisp each side. Remove the onigiri from the pan, press a side or two in sesame seeds to coat (if using), and serve.

NOTE: This works well with frozen cobs, too. Just remember to break your cobs in half before freezing them. After cooking the cobs with the rice, transfer them to the bowl along with the rice, and once they are cool enough to handle, scrape down the sides of the cobs with a knife, gently stir the scrapings into the rice, and proceed with the recipe.

Most fennel recipes use the fennel bulb, full stop.

That's a shame, because the entire plant can be consumed. Bigger stalks can be thinly sliced just like the bulb, and they can also be used to flavor other dishes, like broths (page 129) or the following ice cream recipe. Fronds can be chopped up and used like you would other fresh herbs. They're lovely in a pesto, an egg or potato salad, or as a garnish. If you grow your own fennel, you've got the potential to put a couple more parts of the plant to use if you forgo harvesting the bulb and let it flower and go to seed. You'll be able to collect your own fennel pollen and fennel seeds. The pollen can be sprinkled anywhere you choose: on meat, fish, mushroom dishes—perhaps even ice cream? You may have seen fennel seeds in sausages and stews (those "seeds" are actually fruits, but everyone refers to them as seeds); they also work nicely in cabbage dishes and crackers.

FENNEL STALK ICE CREAM WITH LEMON AND VANILLA BEAN

1½ ounces cream cheese, softened (3 tablespoons)

¼ teaspoon fine-grain sea salt

2 cups whole milk

1 tablespoon plus 1 teaspoon cornstarch

Stalks from 1 fennel bulb

1¼ cups heavy whipping cream

½ cup granulated sugar

2 tablespoons light corn syrup

1 vanilla pod, split and scraped of seeds, both seeds and pod reserved

Zest from 2 lemons, cut off with a paring knife in strips, taking care not to include any pith (or scraping it off with a knife if you do)

I was first introduced to Jeni's Splendid Ice Creams when my older sister, Alison, moved to Columbus to get her PhD. Almost every time I visited we'd go to Jeni's, and my love for the cream cheese–based ice cream was cemented one cold, blustery night when I thought it was too chilly for ice cream—until I read the sign for White Chocolate Evergreen with a Red Currant Garland: "Evergreen is sweet and fragrant with a breath of pine on the finish. White chocolate flecks and handmade red currant sauce are swirled in generously. Like snowflakes on an old-fashioned Christmas tree!"

I was completely sold by the description (and deservedly so—the flavor was incredible), and now I never *ever* pass up an opportunity to visit Jeni's when I'm in town. And thanks to her first cookbook, I now frequently make my own Jeni's-style cream cheese–based ice creams at home. I think her base is less finicky to work with than custard-based ice creams, and I love how easy it is to adapt so you can make your own concoctions, like this refreshing mix of fennel and lemon. It's really important to get just the zest from the lemons; it doesn't take very much pith to end up with bitter ice cream. **MAKES ABOUT A QUART**

1. Whisk the cream cheese and salt together in a medium-size bowl, until blended and smooth, about 1 minute. Set aside.

2. Fill a large bowl with ice.

3. Whisk about 2 tablespoons of the milk together with the cornstarch in a small bowl to make a smooth slurry.

4. Use your fingers to strip the fennel fronds from the stalks (reserve them for another use)—there may be a few fronds left behind, and that's fine. Chop the stalks into 4- or 5-inch lengths —you're just trying to get them to fit in your saucepan.

5. Combine the remaining milk with the cream, sugar, corn syrup, vanilla seeds, and vanilla pod in a large (4-quart or larger) saucepan. Whisk the mixture together and then add the chopped fennel stalks and lemon zest. Bring it to a rolling boil over medium-high heat, and boil for 4 minutes (see box).

6. Remove the mixture from the heat and gradually whisk in the cornstarch slurry. Then return the saucepan to the stovetop, bring it back to a boil over medium-high heat, and cook, stirring, until the mixture is slightly thickened, about 1 minute. Remove the pan from the heat.

7. Scoop out a small amount of the hot milk mixture and gradually whisk it into the cream cheese mixture until smooth. Add the rest of the hot mixture, stirring to combine (including the stalks, zest, and vanilla pod). Pour the mixture into a 1-gallon zip-top freezer bag.

8. Submerge the sealed bag in the bowl of ice and let it stay there until cold, adding more ice as necessary, at least 30 minutes. Strain out the fennel stalks, lemon zest, and vanilla pod. Pour the cold ice cream mixture into an ice cream maker and spin until thick and creamy, about 20 minutes, though the time can vary depending on your machine.

9. Pack the ice cream into a storage container and freeze in the coldest part of your freezer until firm, at least 4 hours.

Unfortunately there are no visual cues in this case—it's important to time it. Very important. As Jeni Britton Bauer once explained in an interview, "More than four [minutes], getting to five and up, it starts to become more like a dulce de leche, like a candied milk, and you evaporate too much water. Less than that, and it's icier."

Bundles of fresh herbs are a cheery sign of spring at the market, but once you get through all the leaves on that herbal bouquet, you're left with a pile of stems . . . that can all be put to good use! The stems from soft herbs (like cilantro, parsley, dill, basil, and chervil—and, although they are not an herb, fennel fronds, too) are really just as versatile as the leaves are: Chop them very fine and use as you would the leaves. Or make herb-infused vinegars (see page 170) with the stems from woody herbs like thyme or rosemary; I tend to stick to one herb at a time, but feel free to go crazy and make your own herb blends. Herb stems can also be used to flavor stock, and the woodier ones can serve as skewers for grilled or roasted vegetables.

As a kid, Hidden Valley Ranch was my salad dressing of choice, so it's no surprise that as an adult I often gravitate toward buttermilk dressings. Basil practically screams warm weather; there's no herb more summery. But since basil is available in grocery stores year-round, whenever you pick some up, don't waste the stems, and you can have a hint of summer on your salads even in the winter. **MAKES ABOUT ⅔ CUP**

1. Combine the basil stems and buttermilk in a small bowl and let steep, covered, in the refrigerator for 8 to 12 hours. Strain and discard the basil stems.

2. Combine ¼ cup of the infused buttermilk, the garlic, mayonnaise, Greek yogurt, a pinch of sea salt, and a few grinds of pepper in a small bowl or glass jar. Shake to combine. Season to taste and thin with extra buttermilk if desired. This dressing will keep up to 3 days in a sealed container in the refrigerator.

JUST-BARELY-BASIL BUTTERMILK DRESSING

½ cup roughly chopped (½ to 1 inch) basil stems (a few errant leaves are fine, too)

½ cup buttermilk

1 medium-size garlic clove, grated on a Microplane or very finely minced

2 tablespoons mayonnaise

2 tablespoons plain Greek yogurt

Fine-grain sea salt

Freshly ground black pepper

If you've never used avocado as a pasta sauce before, I can almost guarantee that it will become a part of your regular meal rotation—the results are so creamy, easy, and delicious. It works well on thin pasta, but if you have a thick pappardelle (or similar) around, that's fine, too. I eat so much cheese on a regular basis that I like this dish as a vegan recipe, but if that's not a concern for you, try a dusting of Parmesan cheese on top when you serve it. Also, the idea is to use up cilantro stems, but there's no need to go out of your way to use *only* stems—a few leaves mixed into the topping would be fine, and you could also use a few leaves to garnish the finished dish. **SERVES 2 OR 3 AS A MAIN DISH**

1. Fill a large pot with generously salted water and bring it to a boil over high heat.

2. While you're waiting for the water to boil, use a small food processor to blend the avocado, lemon juice, and a pinch of salt. Process, taste, and add more salt if necessary.

3. When the water is boiling, add the pasta and cook it according to the package directions.

4. Meanwhile, warm 3 tablespoons of the olive oil in a heavy skillet over medium heat. Add the breadcrumbs and cilantro stems and stir to coat them in oil. If it seems like some breadcrumbs aren't saturated enough, add 1 more tablespoon oil. Cook, stirring occasionally, until the breadcrumbs are lightly browned and crispy, like mini croutons, 8 to 12 minutes. Stir in the lemon zest and remove the pan from the heat.

5. When the pasta is ready, drain it, return it to the pasta pot, and add the pureed avocado mixture, tossing to combine. Plate servings of pasta and top each one with the cilantro stem and breadcrumb mix and a grind of pepper, if desired.

AVOCADO PASTA WITH A CRUNCHY CILANTRO STEM SPRINKLE

1 medium-size or large ripe avocado, pitted and peeled

1 tablespoon freshly squeezed lemon juice

Fine-grain sea salt

8 ounces long, thin pasta (either regular or whole wheat), such as spaghetti, linguine, or bucatini

3 to 4 tablespoons extra virgin olive oil

3/4 cup fresh breadcrumbs (pea to blueberry-size)

3/4 cup very finely chopped cilantro stems

1 teaspoon lemon zest

Freshly ground black pepper (optional)

HERB STEM TAHINI DIP/ DRESSING

⅓ cup very finely chopped soft herb
     stems (errant herb leaves are okay,
     too!)
¼ cup tahini
2 teaspoons soy sauce
1 tablespoon freshly squeezed lemon
     juice
1 teaspoon rice vinegar or apple cider
     vinegar
1 small clove garlic, minced
2 tablespoons hot water
Fine-grain sea salt (optional)

Use whatever mix of herb stems you like and have on hand for this dressing—I like to go heavy on the parsley. Use this as a dip for crudités or thin it out to use as a salad dressing. **MAKES A GENEROUS ½ CUP**

1. Place the herb stems, tahini, soy sauce, lemon juice, vinegar, and garlic in a mini food processor and blend until combined. (Or place them in an appropriate container and use an immersion blender.)

2. Add the hot water and blend again until smooth. Taste and adjust seasoning; it might need a touch more lemon juice or a little salt, especially if you used low-sodium soy sauce. Use as a dip or spread, or add a little more hot water and blend again to thin it out for a salad dressing. It will keep as a dip or dressing for up to 3 days in a sealed container in the refrigerator.

PARSLEY STEM TABBOULEH

If you are a tabbouleh fan, you may have strong opinions on the components and their ratio. Feel free to play with the ingredients: more or less bulgur, green onions instead of sweet onion, flat-leaf parsley instead of curly, the addition of cucumber, etc. The only nonnegotiable with this tabbouleh is knife skills—the parsley stems have to be very (very!) finely chopped for this recipe to work. If they aren't, they'll throw off the texture of the salad, and you'll curse my name for ruining your batch of tabbouleh.

You'll often find bulgur labeled by grind; I like to use Bob's Red Mill bulgur, which is medium grind (#2). Tabbouleh is often made with fine grind (#1) bulgur, but it can be hard to find in some areas. If you do use fine grind, follow preparation instructions on the package, as it won't take as long to soak as medium grind does. I like to grate the onion, because it almost turns to mush and nicely spreads out throughout the salad, but if you'd rather not dirty one more utensil (this is a labor-intensive dish), you can finely chop it instead. **SERVES 4 AS A SIDE DISH**

¼ cup whole grain bulgur
  (see headnote)

¾ cup boiling water

1 big bunch curly parsley

2 tablespoons finely chopped mint
  leaves

1 small sweet or white onion, grated
  (about ¼ cup grated)

1 plum tomato, chopped
  (about ⅓ cup chopped),
  seeds and any juice reserved

1 tablespoon lemon zest

⅓ cup freshly squeezed lemon juice
  (from 2 medium-size to large lemons,
  any extra juice reserved)

¼ cup extra virgin olive oil

¾ teaspoon fine-grain sea salt

¼ teaspoon cayenne pepper

1. Place the bulgur in a small bowl, and pour ¼ cup of the boiling water over it. Let it stand for 1 hour, and then drain any remaining liquid.

2. Strip the parsley leaves from the stems (little stems are okay to keep) and chop the stems very finely (you'll have about ½ cup)—discard the very bottoms of the stems if they look brown or dried out. Place them in a small bowl, pour the remaining ½ cup boiling water over them, and let stand for 15 minutes, until softened slightly but still crunchy. Drain the excess liquid. (To minimize dishes, wait until the bulgur has finished soaking and move it to the medium-size bowl that you'll assemble the tabbouleh in. Then reuse the small bowl for the parsley stems.)

3. Meanwhile, finely chop the parsley leaves (you'll have about 2½ cups) and place them in a medium-size bowl along with the mint leaves, grated onion, and chopped tomato. Drain the softened chopped stems and add them to the mix, along with the presoaked bulgur. Stir to combine.

4. Place the reserved tomato seeds and juice, lemon zest and juice, olive oil, salt, and cayenne pepper in a small bowl and whisk to combine. Pour about two thirds of the dressing on the bulgur mixture and toss to coat. Taste and adjust seasoning as necessary, adding more dressing, more of the reserved lemon juice, or more salt. Serve immediately or let the tabbouleh hang out in the refrigerator for a few hours. Store extras (of the dressing or the tabbouleh) in an airtight container in the refrigerator.

JAM

One of my dads, Greg (find his hot toddy recipe on page 164), doesn't let a jar of jam get recycled until every last drop has been scraped out. The rest of us are more likely to give up on the last lingering bits clinging to the sides and bottom, but they can be rescued (without undue effort on your part). No need to measure out an exact tablespoon of jam for either of these recipes—just eyeball what's left in the jar.

This section is also really a ploy to introduce ginger marmalade into your life if you aren't already a fan. Find it in the international aisle of your grocery store or a store that sells British and Scottish foods, and then slather it on toast, use it on peanut butter and jelly sandwiches, and then use the dregs in salad dressings, marinades, and as a dipping sauce for soba noodles (page 105).

While living in Japan, we made one trip to Tokyo, and I wanted to make the most of our limited time there. Two nonnegotiables on my list were both movie-related: (1) getting a cocktail at the New York Bar in the Park Hyatt (definitely worth it for the views, especially worth it if you're a fan of *Lost in Translation*) and (2) going to the Nishi-Azabu location of Gonpachi (the restaurant has multiple locations in the city, but the interior of this one inspired the set for a famous fight scene in *Kill Bill*).

I'd recommend a trip to Gonpachi even if you're not a *Kill Bill* fan for the good food at reasonable prices (and cheap drink deals). It's also one of the places where I clearly remember eating cold soba noodles with dipping sauce, a popular summertime food in Japan.

Just like miso soup (page 161), the base for the dipping sauce is generally made with dashi—broth made from steeping kombu and bonito flakes, often overnight. This is a quickie version that, while it isn't traditional, is very tasty all the same. **SERVES 3 OR 4**

1. Place a medium-size pot over medium heat and add the oil. Once the oil has warmed up, add the fresh ginger, garlic, and the white parts of the green onions, and sauté, stirring occasionally, until the onions are nearly translucent, about 5 minutes. Add 1 cup water to the pan, scrape up any bits that stuck, and remove from the heat.

2. Add the tablespoon of very hot water to the marmalade jar. Replace the lid and vigorously shake, then use a fork or small spatula to scrape around the sides and release all of the lingering marmalade bits. Add this mixture and the soy sauce to the pan and stir to combine. Transfer the dipping sauce to a serving bowl, cover, and place in the fridge.

3. Fill a large pot with water and bring to a boil. Add the soba noodles, and give them a quick stir to submerge them all. Let the water return to a boil, then reduce the heat a little to keep the water at a simmer. Let the noodles cook according to package directions, probably between 5 and 8 minutes. Meanwhile, ready a colander in the sink. Once the noodles

SOBA NOODLES WITH GINGER MARMALADE DIPPING SAUCE

1 tablespoon untoasted sesame oil
  (or other neutral-flavored oil)
1 tablespoon finely minced fresh ginger
1 garlic clove, minced
5 or 6 green onions, white and green
  parts separated and thinly sliced
1 tablespoon ginger marmalade,
  in the jar (See page 103. Substitute
  any citrus-y marmalade if you can't
  find ginger, but do try to find it!)
1 tablespoon very hot water
½ cup soy sauce
1 package (9 or 10 ounces) soba noodles
  (look for a high percentage of
  buckwheat flour)
Toasted sesame seeds, for garnish
  (optional, see page 22)

are cooked, drain them and then run cold water over them while carefully lifting and separating the noodles, and gently rubbing them with your fingers. This is cooling down the noodles, yes, but it's also washing off the excess starch, thus preventing a gummy pile of noodles. Let them sit for a minute for additional water to drip off. (If you'd like to chill the noodles, transfer them to a covered bowl in the refrigerator until they've reached your desired temperature.)

If I want to serve this to more people as an appetizer, I'll make individual (large) bite-size nests of noodles on a serving platter. That way it's easy for people to pick up little bundles, ready for dipping in the sauce.

4. To serve, divide the soba noodles among individual bowls, sprinkle each with the sliced green onion tops, and sesame seeds, if using, and either pour some of the sauce over each bowl, or let each diner pick up noodles with chopsticks and dunk them in the sauce.

This dressing recipe is intended to be made right in the jam jar—fewer dishes to wash!—with the last bits of jam clinging to the sides and the bottom. No need to measure out that there's a tablespoon of jam left—just eyeball it.

This is especially good as a dressing for spinach salad with strawberries or other fresh berries. Experiment with other types of jam too! **MAKES ABOUT ½ CUP**

1. Add the hot water to the jam jar. Replace the lid and vigorously shake, then use a fork or small spatula to scrape around the sides and release all of the lingering jam bits.

2. Add the vinegar, shallot, lemon juice, olive oil, and sea salt to the jar and vigorously shake again to combine. This dressing will keep for up to 3 days in a sealed container in the refrigerator.

STRAWBERRY JAM BALSAMIC VINAIGRETTE

1 tablespoon very hot water

1 tablespoon strawberry jam, in the jar (see headnote)

1 tablespoon balsamic vinegar

1 tablespoon minced shallot

2 teaspoons freshly squeezed lemon juice

3 tablespoons extra virgin olive oil

Pinch of fine-grain sea salt

Some people think we're riding a kale bubble that's soon to burst, leaving us to all move on to the next hip vegetable, whatever that may be, but I'd like to disagree. Kale is here to stay, and not just because it's super nutritious, but also because it's versatile. It's at its best during the coldest months of the year, when fresh vegetable selections are slimmer, and most importantly, it tastes good. (Full disclosure: I also own a kale sweatshirt. I'm all in for kale.) Whichever variety of kale you're partial to, know that the tough stalks can be just as enjoyable as the leaves. Try pickling or sautéing them—if you're going to be sautéing the leaves, cut the stems into small pieces and start cooking them first before adding the leaves.

KALE STEM HUMMUS

Making the hummus from London chefs and restauranteurs Yotam Ottolenghi and Sami Tamimi's book *Jerusalem* for the first time was a revelation. I never knew that homemade hummus could be so smooth. It's due to cooking the soaked chickpeas for a short period of time with baking soda, and this technique provides the foundation of every hummus I've made since. I prefer less tahini than they call for, but the one ingredient not to mess with is the dried chickpeas—this is one instance where using dried beans instead of canned makes a big difference.

Despite how tough and woody kale stems are, they blend in surprisingly well. Depending on the depth of color in your kale stems and how long you cook them, your hummus could stay a standard hummus-beige or have a green tint or be somewhere in-between—any shade is okay and equally delicious. **SERVES 6 TO 8**

1 cup dried chickpeas

1 teaspoon baking soda

Stems from 1 bunch kale (see Note)

3 garlic cloves, minced

⅔ cup tahini

1 teaspoon fine-grain sea salt

⅔ cup freshly squeezed lemon juice

Ice water

Extra virgin olive oil, for serving

1. The night before you plan on making the hummus, put the chickpeas in a large bowl, cover them with at least twice their volume of water, and leave them to soak overnight at room temperature.

2. The next day, drain and rinse the chickpeas. Put them along with the baking soda in a medium-size pot over high heat. Stir constantly for about 3 minutes. Add 6 to 8 cups water, until the chickpeas are covered by a few inches, and bring to a boil. Reduce the heat to medium, cover the pot, and simmer until the chickpeas are very tender—45 to 60 minutes—checking on them occasionally to skim off any foam on the surface. Skim off any chickpea skins that float up as well, but there's no need to try to remove the skins if they don't come off. They were softened by the baking soda and will blend smoothly into the hummus.

3. Meanwhile, fill another medium-size pot with water and bring to a boil. Add the kale stems and cook until they are very tender, 30 to 45 minutes. Drain them.

4. Place the kale stems, garlic, and tahini in a food processor and process, scraping down the sides as necessary, until well blended.

5. Once the chickpeas are cooked, drain them, add them to the kale stem mixture in the food processor along with the salt and lemon juice, and process until smooth. Add 2 tablespoons ice water and process until the hummus is very smooth and creamy, about 5 minutes. Add up to 2 additional tablespoons ice water, one at a time, and process again as necessary.

6. To serve, spoon into a shallow bowl and drizzle with olive oil.

7. The hummus can be stored in the refrigerator for 3 to 5 days or frozen for up to 3 months. After thawing frozen hummus, you might need to adjust the seasoning—taste and add salt and lemon juice as necessary.

NOTE: Try this hummus with other scraps too, like Swiss chard stalks or cauliflower cores. Follow the same cooking method as outlined in Step 3, boiling until very tender, 15 to 30 minutes.

Most recipes for leeks call for using only the white part—the very bottom few inches. That leaves a lot of the plant left over! You can always toss the green leek tops in your freezer for stock (page 129), but they're also fine to eat just as they are. The following recipe uses both the light green stalk and the dark green leaves. Cut away any dry ends of the leaves, and if you have a couple of outermost leaves that look or feel slightly spongy, save those for stock or the compost pile. Much like leafy greens (see page xix), leeks and other alliums with greens attached need to be washed really well, as they can hide a lot of dirt. I like to split leeks in half lengthwise and hold them under running water, being careful to clean out between all of their layers and the crooks where the leaves bend out.

My first experience with cacio e pepe was a mistake. I saw it on a menu, thought, *Pasta, cheese, pepper? Sold.* I ordered by pointing at it, too afraid of garbling the pronunciation and revealing my inexperience, but I shouldn't have worried. They didn't know what they were doing either. What arrived on my plate was a gummy, gooey mess with nary a speck of pepper to be seen. I took a couple bites, then moved the rest of it around with a fork, like I'd regressed to childhood and was trying to convince my parents that I was eating. Then I gave up on the dish.

The true error was not in my (persistent, misguided) fear of making a verbal gaffe, nor in the restaurant's bungling of the dish (maybe it was a bad night?), but in my decision to write off cacio e pepe as a result. Until, that is, I had a good—no, stellar—version of it at Maialino, in New York City, where I realized what I'd been missing out on. I've continued to order it at restaurants, but I've also learned that it's an easy dish that can and should be made at home. Plus, thanks to Food52er Sara G., I've picked up on the idea of adding a little dose of green to the dish. She adds radish or baby turnip greens to hers, but I like adding thinly cut lengths of leek tops to mine.

SERVES 2 OR 3

1. Fill a large pot with salted water (use 2 or 3 three-finger pinches of salt—it should taste like the sea) and bring it to a boil over medium-high heat.

2. Meanwhile, stack a couple of leek lengths on top of one another and make narrow cuts down the length of them, like you're turning them into linguini. Once you get the hang of this, you can make your stack a little higher. Don't stress out about it too much; they won't all look perfect—it's fine.

3. When the water is boiling, add the pasta and give it a stir. Take note of the instructions on the package; you'll be subtracting 2 minutes from the cooking time. One minute before the pasta is done (so 3 minutes before the time on the package), add the shredded leek tops.

4. Drain the pasta and leek tops, reserving 1 cup of the cooking water.

LEEK TOP CACIO E PEPE

1 leek top, split in half (see page 111) and cut into 6-inch lengths

6 ounces bucatini or spaghetti

3 tablespoons extra virgin olive oil

2 teaspoons freshly ground black pepper

1 cup grated Grana Padano or Parmigiano Reggiano cheese

⅓ cup grated pecorino Romano cheese

5. Return the empty pot to the same burner and turn the heat to medium. Add the olive oil and pepper to the pot; let it sit until it smells fragrant, 30 seconds to 1 minute.

6. Add the drained pasta and leek tops to the pot, and using tongs, toss everything around to coat. Add ¼ cup of the reserved pasta water to the pot, sprinkle on about half of the cheese (you'll end up with cheese clumps if you dump it all in one pile), and, using the tongs, toss to coat and melt the cheese. Repeat this step with another ¼ cup pasta water and the rest of the cheese.

7. You should now have a silky sauce coating all of the pasta and leek tops (the tops might require a little more tong action to distribute them evenly). If not, add a little more pasta water and toss everything again, then serve and eat immediately.

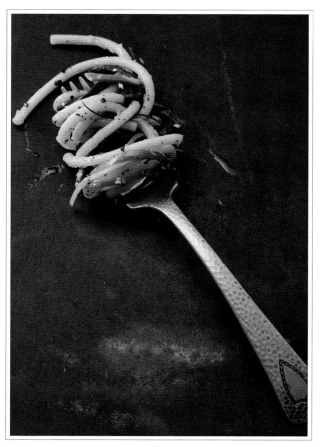

The scraps of melons—cantaloupe, honeydew, and watermelon being the most common—include more than just the seeds. The pulp (in some cases) and the rind are typically discarded after the sweet flesh is scooped out. Seeds can be roasted—yes, even those watermelon seeds—and pulp can be pureed and added to smoothies and chilled melon gazpacho.

The white inner rind of watermelon is crunchy and mild in flavor, making it ripe (or not! eh, eh?) for use in savory or sweet dishes, from pickles to jam. I've had the best luck with larger melons, as smaller watermelons often seem to have a thinner, more fibrous white layer of rind.

WATERMELON RIND—LIME GRANITA WITH BASIL WHIPPED CREAM

10 to 15 basil leaves, plus more for garnish

1 cup heavy whipping cream

4 cups pureed watermelon rind
   (see headnote)

1 cup freshly squeezed lime juice

1 cup simple syrup (page 32)

2 teaspoons granulated sugar
   (or more, to taste)

Watermelon rinds are often pickled, but I wanted to find a sweet use for them. Their refreshing wateriness naturally lends itself to granita, which I like paired with an herbal, just-barely-sweetened dollop of whipped cream.

To get pureed watermelon rind, simply peel off and discard the outer green rind of the watermelon, and put chunks of the white rind in a blender. It might need some nudging with a wooden spoon (when the blender isn't running!) to get it going, but the white rind is juicy enough that it should easily blend. If your watermelon doesn't produce 4 cups of puree, simply halve or quarter the recipe.

Plan ahead for this recipe! You'll need at least 12 hours from start to finish, and you'll want to check to make sure your baking dish fits into your freezer before you pour the liquid into it. If it doesn't, it's okay to use a smaller, deeper container; just know that the mixture will take longer to freeze. Depending on the color of your watermelon, and how much of the flesh is left clinging to the rind, your granita will turn out differently, from pale green to yellow to pink. **MAKES ENOUGH GRANITA FOR A CROWD**

1. At least 8 hours before you plan to make the granita, preferably the night before, rip the basil leaves into pieces (not tiny, just in halves or thirds), combine them with the heavy cream, and store in a covered container in the refrigerator for 8 to 12 hours.

2. Strain out the basil leaves from the infused cream and return it to the refrigerator until you're ready to whip it.

3. Place the watermelon rind puree, lime juice, and simple syrup in a large bowl and stir to combine.

4. Pour the mixture into a 9-by-13-inch cake pan (or similar baking dish) and place in the freezer until partially frozen, about 1 hour. Scrape with a fork to fluff up the mixture into icy shards. Return to the freezer and repeat the scrape-and-fluff process every 30 to 60 minutes until the mixture is fully frozen, about 4 hours total.

5. Shortly before you're ready to serve the granita, make the whipped cream. Place the infused cream and granulated sugar in a medium-size bowl, and using a hand mixer on low speed, whip until the cream thickens enough not to splatter. Increase the speed to medium-high and whip until it's thickened to your liking. Taste and adjust the sweetness level as desired.

6. Serve the granita in bowls with basil leaves and dollops of whipped cream on top.

ROASTED CANTALOUPE SEEDS WITH CHILI AND LIME

Seeds from 1 or 2 cantaloupes,
  rinsed and dried
1 teaspoon extra virgin olive oil
1 teaspoon freshly squeezed lime juice
Scant ¼ teaspoon chili powder
Scant ¼ teaspoon fine-grain sea salt

I love roasted pumpkin seeds, but you don't have to wait until autumn to enjoy a snack of crunchy seeds. The seeds of all members of the Cucurbitaceae family are edible, so while some might not be worth the effort (I'm looking at you, cucumber seeds), you can try roasting the seeds of other types of melons, winter squashes (page 145), and even overgrown baseball bat–size zucchini. **MAKES ¼ TO ½ CUP**

1. Preheat the oven to 325°F.

2. On a rimmed baking sheet, toss the seeds with the olive oil, lime juice, chili powder, and salt. Spread them out into a single layer.

3. Roast the seeds, stirring once or twice, until they are golden brown, 20 to 30 minutes. Remove from the oven and let them cool down on the baking sheet. They'll continue to crisp up as they cool. Keep them for up to 2 weeks in a zip-top bag or a sealed container on the counter.

Overnight oats make for an especially easy breakfast that doesn't take much time or effort—just mix your ingredients in a bowl, divide into containers, and wait until morning. In cooler weather, I often like to heat up the finished oats, but in the summer I like eating them cold, straight from the refrigerator. The melon pulp and lemon zest make this version extra refreshing.

I generally use a spoon to scoop the whole pulpy, seedy center of the melon into a 2-cup glass measuring cup and then use my fingers to separate out the seeds (save them for roasting, page 118), but you could also use a strainer set over a bowl. Don't worry if you end up with less or more pulp from your melon, just adjust the amount of milk you use so you end up using about 1¼ cups liquid total. Feel free to try topping this with other fresh fruit as well, like bananas or strawberries. **SERVES 2**

1. Place the oats, melon juice and pulp, milk, hemp seeds (if using), chia seeds, lemon zest, vanilla extract, and salt in a medium-size bowl and mix to combine.

2. Divide into 2 bowls, cover with plastic wrap (or use containers with lids, like glass jars), and place in the refrigerator until morning, or for at least 8 hours.

3. When you're ready to eat, top each bowl with half of the blueberries and a drizzle of honey.

CANTALOUPE PULP OVERNIGHT OATS WITH LEMON AND BLUEBERRIES

1 cup old-fashioned rolled oats

Pulp and juice from the seedy center of 1 cantaloupe, about ½ cup once the seeds are removed

¾ cup cashew milk (or other non-dairy or dairy milk)

1 tablespoon hemp seeds (optional)

1 tablespoon chia seeds

1 teaspoon lemon zest

½ teaspoon vanilla extract

Pinch of fine-grain sea salt

½ cup blueberries, for serving

1 tablespoon honey, for serving

Mushroom stems can usually be chopped right up and cooked along with the caps. If you've been tossing them, take note—it's only a matter of remembering to incorporate them into a dish. (Chop the stems more finely than the caps since they may take longer to cook.) The base may need to be trimmed—check for woodiness. You don't want to use any part of the stem that feels hardened or dried out. If you're using mushrooms in raw form, like in a salad, save the stems for another use. They will work beautifully if pureed in soups or broths, and if you are making stuffed mushroom caps, the addition of finely chopped stems will only enhance whatever stuffing you are making. Compound butters, like the one on the next page, are quick and easy to make, and they provide a great home for all sorts of odds and ends, especially extra herbs that might otherwise go to waste.

The magical thing about compound butters is that you can fold in nearly anything, and you'll come out with a delicious flavored spread that will heighten any dish—be it a piece of toast or a roasted chicken. The earthiness of mushrooms is an ideal complement to rich, creamy butter, but there are many delicious combinations possible. Try any extra herb, finely chopped, either by itself or combined with other herbs; citrus zest, on its own or with an herb or honey; finely grated cheese; pesto; any combination of spices or condiments, like harissa, garam marsala, freshly ground pepper, and mustard seeds; or roasted garlic. For a sweet twist, mix in jam dregs, add cinnamon and brown sugar, or try cardamom and vanilla sugar (see page 165).

Compound butters also store well in the freezer: Wrap them into a log shape in waxed or parchment paper and then again in plastic wrap. **MAKES A GENEROUS ⅓ CUP**

MUSHROOM STEM COMPOUND BUTTER

Mushroom stems from 1 package
   (8 ounces) of cremini or
   white button mushrooms
5 tablespoons unsalted butter,
   softened
1 small shallot, finely chopped
   (about 1 heaping tablespoon)
½ rounded teaspoon chopped,
   fresh thyme
½ teaspoon brandy (optional)
Fine-grain sea salt

1. Check the very ends of the mushroom stems and slice off any parts that look dry. Then finely chop the stems. You should have somewhere around ½ cup chopped.

2. Place 1 tablespoon of the butter in a medium-size pan over medium heat. Once it's melted, add the shallot and sauté until tender and translucent, 3 to 5 minutes.

3. Add the mushrooms, thyme, and brandy (if you're using it) to the shallot, and sauté until the mushrooms are fully cooked and softened, 4 to 5 minutes. Turn off the heat and let cool.

4. Fold the remaining 4 tablespoons butter into the cooled mushroom mixture, either right in the pan or in a small bowl. Don't worry if you weren't patient and the mushrooms are still hot enough to melt the butter—it will firm right back up again in the refrigerator. I like to store it in a ramekin and keep it in the fridge for 3 or 4 days for spreading on toast (let it come back to room temperature first for easier spreading).

CLEAN *out the* **CRISPER**

Frittatas are one of my go-to weeknight dinners. This dish comes together quickly, is easier than quiche (no need to make a crust), and this version is less finicky than a stovetop frittata (you're not moving the eggs around at all; the oven does all the work). Plus it makes use of any straggler cooked or raw vegetables and nubs of cheese you have lingering in the refrigerator.

Important: If you have only nonfat dairy in the house, skip the ⅓ cup dairy! A fat-free option won't do anything for your frittata in terms of flavor or texture, so it's better to omit it entirely.

OVEN FRITTATA

SERVES 4 TO 6

Small knob of unsalted butter

8 large eggs

⅓ cup liquid (or liquid-ish) dairy (plain yogurt, sour cream, milk, and so on—see headnote)

⅔ cup shredded or crumbled cheese

½ teaspoon fine-grain sea salt

Freshly ground black pepper

Up to 3 cups roughly chopped vegetables of your choice (see Note)

Extra virgin olive oil (see Note)

1. Preheat the oven to 350°F.

2. Grease a 9-inch pie pan or oven-safe skillet with the butter.

3. Place the eggs, your choice of dairy, and the cheese in a medium-size bowl. Whisk together and add the salt and as much pepper as you'd like.

4. Scatter the vegetables in the pie plate and then pour the egg mixture over the top. Bake until the eggs are just set, 15 to 20 minutes. Note that the top won't brown, which I prefer, but if you'd like a toasty top layer, pop the baked frittata under the broiler for a moment.

NOTE: You can use any combination of cooked and raw vegetables here, just be sure to sauté any raw veggies in a bit of olive oil or butter first. They should be fully cooked before you add them in Step 4.

Peanuts are actually legumes, while tree nuts include cashews, hazelnuts, pecans, and many other types. Since they are often grouped together under the category "nuts," both types are found here. Nuts might not seem like they have much in the way of useable scraps, but in fact they do. Peanut shells still hold a surprising amount of peanut flavor. Nut pulp is what's left over after making nut milks, like almond milk, or my favorite: cashew milk. To do so, nuts are soaked (generally overnight), then drained, blended with fresh water, and strained—using cheesecloth or a nut milk bag. Making your own nut milks produces better nut milks than you can get from any supermarket shelf, but it also produces a lot of leftover nut pulp. You'll often see suggestions to use these scraps in baked goods, but they have savory applications as well, like in onigirazu (page 127) and in a faux tuna salad (page 128).

I was introduced to the idea of making cheese at home when I came across blogger and cookbook author Jennifer Perillo's recipe for Creamy Homemade Ricotta on Food52. If you haven't tried it before, it might sound intimidating, but really it couldn't be easier. When I made it for the first time and the curds started to separate, it felt like magic—so much that I did a little dance around the kitchen and pulled everyone over to take a peek for themselves. The first taste was equally magical, and I wondered why it took me so long to try it.

Pot cheese might induce a giggle or two, but the name is simply due to the fact that it's made in a pot. It's creamy, sometimes a little crumbly, and not as dry as the better-known make-at-home cheese, farmers' cheese. I like to add small blobs of it to composed salads, dollop it in soups, and smear it on crackers or crostini. When you think about where you'll use it, take note that it is a very salty cheese!

The ingredients in this recipe differ from Jennifer's, but at times the instructions closely mirror her method—because it works. I found it easiest to locate roasted, salted in-shell peanuts, but if you get unsalted peanuts, just add ¼ teaspoon fine-grain sea salt. If you don't have cheesecloth, a (clean) tea towel will work; it just might need more time to drain. The leftover whey can be used in soup or bread—it will be extremely salty, so take care to adjust the salt in the recipe. **MAKES A GENEROUS CUP**

1. Combine the peanut shells, heavy cream, and milk in a medium-size bowl. Cover and refrigerate for about 8 hours, stirring once or twice if you think about it.

2. Line a mesh strainer with a couple of layers of cheesecloth, and set it over another medium-size bowl. Pour the peanut shell-and-cream mixture into the lined strainer. Once all of the liquid drains through, transfer the liquid to a medium-size pot—it's okay that the liquid will be flecked with tiny

PEANUT SHELL– INFUSED POT CHEESE

3 to 4 cups peanut shells from roasted, salted in-shell peanuts

2 cups heavy whipping cream

1 cup whole milk

2 tablespoons freshly squeezed lemon juice

bits of the peanut's papery inner seed coats. Discard the peanut shells. Rinse out the bowl, strainer, and cheesecloth—you're going to reuse them—and set them up again as before.

3. Add the lemon juice to the pot and heat over medium heat, bringing the mixture to a simmer. (You're aiming for gentle bubbles—too much heat and you'll get a rolling boil and scalded milk—so turn down the heat if your stovetop runs hot.)

4. Once you start to see curds separating, turn down the heat to the lowest setting, cook for 2 more minutes, then remove from the heat. Shift the pot to a cool (unlit) burner and allow it to sit for 45 minutes to an hour. If you're having trouble telling whether or not curds are forming, dip a spoon in the pot—it will make it easier to see the little white specks of separating curds. Resist the urge to stir the pot.

5. Slowly pour the contents of the pot into the cheesecloth and let the cheese drain until it reaches a consistency you like. This could be as little as 20 minutes for a very wet cheese or a few hours for a very firm cheese—for the latter, pull the sides of the cheesecloth up to loosely cover the cheese and let it drain in the refrigerator.

6. Store the cheese in a covered container in the refrigerator for up to 3 days.

*O*nigirazu are kind of like a mash-up between *onigiri* (rice ball, see page 91), rolled sushi, and a sandwich. If you aren't adept at rolling sushi, onigirazu gives you a similar flavor profile, but is easier to master. Typically, onigirazu starts with a sheet of nori, then has a layer of rice, then other fillings, then rice again, with the nori folded up around it. This recipe uses the same principles, but substitutes cashew pulp (or other nut pulp) for the rice. I've listed one of my favorite filling combinations—inspired by a raw sushi roll my friend Corinna Borden once made me—but this is a very flexible recipe, so try different fillings and make it your own! If you haven't worked with nori before, it's dried seaweed that's pressed into thin sheets. You can find it in the international aisle of grocery stores, at Asian markets, or online.

Onigirazu made with rice can be made ahead of time and will hold up for a half a day or so, making them ideal for packed lunches. Fresh nut pulps, on the other hand, tend to have more moisture in them than rice, so the nori will start to disintegrate faster, meaning this version is best prepared shortly before you plan to eat it. **MAKES 2 "SANDWICHES"**

CASHEW PULP ONIGIRAZU

2 sheets nori

2 teaspoons white miso paste

1 cup cashew pulp, left over from making cashew milk

Pickled root vegetable slices (like turnips, beets, or carrots, store-bought or homemade, page 58)

A generous handful of sprouts or microgreens (see box)

½ avocado, thinly sliced

Soy sauce

1. Lay out two pieces of plastic wrap—each just larger than the nori—side by side on your counter, and top each one with a sheet of nori.

2. Gently spread 1 teaspoon of the miso paste around in a circular shape in the middle of each sheet of nori with your fingers or the back of a spoon. Place ¼ cup of the cashew pulp in the middle of the sheet on top of the miso paste, and flatten it slightly. Top with a layer each of pickled vegetables, sprouts or microgreens, and avocado slices. Add a sprinkle—just a few drops!—of soy sauce, then top each one with another ¼ cup cashew pulp.

What's the difference between sprouts and microgreens? Sprouts are the first stage of germination. You'll see a little sprout coming out of the seed (or bean, grain, or nut) and maybe some root hairs—the entire thing is edible! Seeds that have sprouted and have been allowed to grow a little more (in soil or another growing medium) are microgreens. They are tiny plants that are clipped near the base of their stems. Look for either at well-stocked grocery stores, health food stores, or your local farmers market.

3. Fold the corners of each nori sheet into the middle to form a rough square. Then wrap the squares with the plastic wrap to tighten them up. The square will become more circular in shape—that's okay!

4. Let the sandwich sit for a few minutes to allow the nori to soften slightly and form around the filling. I pick it up and eat it as is, but you can also slice the sandwich in half—just do so carefully, as the filling might start to spill out. Serve right away.

CASHEW PULP "TUNA" SALAD

2 teaspoons freshly squeezed lemon
    juice
1 teaspoon cornichon brine
    (or dill pickle brine)
½ teaspoon soy sauce
½ teaspoon Dijon mustard
3 tablespoons mayonnaise
1½ cups cashew pulp, left over from
    making cashew milk
1 small shallot, minced
    (about 1 tablespoon)
2 teaspoons minced dill
1 tablespoon chopped cornichons
    (or dill pickles, in a pinch)
1 tablespoon nutritional yeast

I like the texture and mild flavor of cashew pulp for this recipe, but if you have other types of leftover nut pulps, feel free to experiment. Nutritional yeast is an inactive yeast that's dried into a flake or powder form (either one works here); this isn't a type of yeast that can help leaven bread, but it does add a savory, slightly cheesy flavor to dishes—try it sprinkled on popcorn. The cheesiness doesn't come through in this salad, it just rounds out the flavors. Look for nutritional yeast in the natural foods section of grocery stores, in health food stores, or online.

Serve as you would traditional tuna salad—either in sandwiches, with crackers, or scooped on top of a green salad. **SERVES 2**

1. Whisk together the lemon juice, cornichon brine, soy sauce, mustard, and mayonnaise in a medium-size bowl.

2. Add the cashew pulp, shallot, dill, cornichons, and nutritional yeast and stir to combine. Taste and adjust for seasoning.

Stocks and Broths

Stocks and Broths are the dumping grounds (the good kind) for all of the little scraps you can't figure out what to do with. Yes, you can make stock with whole vegetables, but for the most part I prefer to use as much of the vegetable as possible and save the scrappiest of scraps for stock.

VEGETABLE BROTH, FROZEN OR FRESH

For vegetable broth, I keep a zip-top bag (or a reusable container) in the freezer and add scraps as I have them. Once the bag is full, I simply dump them in a large pot, cover them with water, add a bay leaf, and simmer for an hour, adding a couple of peppercorns, a splash of white wine if I have it, and salt to taste near the end of the cooking time, if desired (start with a big pinch and add more if needed). The resulting liquid will change with the seasons, depending on what's in the bag, but you can also create specialized separate versions as well. For instance, in the summertime, collect corn cobs and husks in their own bag in the freezer for corn stock (depending on the size of your pot, you might want to break the cobs in half first), which I like to use in risotto or to make a corn soup extra corny.

If you aren't starting with frozen, sauté aromatics like onion, garlic, celery, and carrots first to give your broth a greater depth

of flavor, and always add in a Parmesan rind if you have one. I keep a separate freezer bag full of Parmesan rinds too, because they're not only good for adding to other types of stocks and soups; you can make Parmesan broth, with or without adding things like onion, celery, and carrots—I like either straight Parmesan or Parmesan with an onion. Aim for about a pound of Parmesan rinds with 10 to 12 cups water, and again simmer for an hour. It's perfect in simple soups, in a pot of beans, or as braising liquid for vegetables. (I stick with Parmigiano Reggiano and Grana Padano rinds for broth and save others for Cheese Rind Fromage Fort (page 68), but the rinds from any hard cheese would work.)

A MEATIER STOCK

To make stock from bones, either save them (after you roast a chicken or fish), or ask your butcher for bones (whether beef, pork, poultry, or fish). For bone-based stocks, if you're using raw bones, consider roasting the bones first for additional flavor (try 400°F for 30 minutes, and don't forget to scrape up any bits stuck to the bottom of the pan—that's flavor!). Then, in a large, heavy pot, cover the bones with water, add a tablespoon or two of apple cider vinegar (or other vinegar), and keep the temperature just below a simmer—a few bubbles are okay, but you don't want it boiling—for as little as a few hours and up to a day (this is where a slow cooker comes in handy). Obviously, the longer you cook them, the more flavorful the stock—once you reach the 1-day mark you're getting into bone broth territory. There's no magical difference between regular broth and bone broth, just time. Bone broth is generally cooked for 24 hours, though sometimes even longer; but once the bones start to crumble, you've gotten all of the flavor—and nutrients—out of them that you're going to.

For these meaty stocks, less is more, in terms of vegetables—this isn't the place to dump in your bag of scraps. Keep it simple with onions, garlic, and a few peppercorns, all added in the last hour of cooking. For chicken stock consider adding a knob of ginger or some spent lemons along with an onion. Some people include vegetables with the bones for the whole time, but I follow Michael Ruhlman's advice that any longer than an hour, and the vegetables are completely breaking down and merely absorbing stock (that you'll then lose when you strain them out) rather than adding flavor.

Once your stock is done, strain it, either with a mesh colander or a cheesecloth-lined colander, let it cool down, and then store it in the refrigerator for up to 4 days or the freezer (portioned into cup-size allotments if desired), where it will keep for up to 6 months.

ITEMS TO AVOID OR USE IN MODERATION

Strong and Bitter Vegetables: Things like cabbage, brussels sprouts, cauliflower, kohlrabi, and bitter greens all have the potential to overwhelm a stock or make it bitter. (Are you picking up a theme? If the vegetable is a member of the Brassica family, it might not be great for stock.) For some vegetables, you might consider keeping a separate stock stash to make a dedicated stock, like asparagus ends to make asparagus stock for soup.

Squash: The peels from winter squash can add flavor to stock, but don't add the flesh—it's too starchy. If you're not using the seeds (for roasting, page 145, for example) or the webbing (in scones, page 143), you can use them along with the peels to create a squash broth that's perfect in squash soups or risotto.

Onion and Garlic Skins: I occasionally include a small amount of papery onion and/or garlic skins, but the issues are twofold: (1) too many can make your stock bitter and (2) onion skins (of any shade) will color your stock.

Potatoes: Whether you're using just the peels or the whole tuber, potatoes will make your stock murky. So if you're aiming for a clear, golden vegetable stock, skip them. If you'd like a vegetable stock with a little more substance and don't care that it will be cloudy, proceed.

Beets: Like onion skins, beets (the root, peel, and/or stems) will have an impact on the color of your stock. If you don't mind the resulting pink hue, feel free to include them.

Dill pickle brine is an incredibly useful scrap—the salty, amped-up vinegar is a powerful dish brightener. That also goes for its saline kin, such as olive, caper, cornichon, pepperoncini brines, and the like. Once you start using the salty leftovers of various pickled and preserved vegetables—in salad dressings, cocktails, marinades, to make more pickles—you might find yourself running out of the liquid before you even finish the actual contents of the jar.

Dill pickle brine is an essential part of a pickleback—a shot of whiskey chased by a shot of pickle juice—but its salty tang is welcome in other drinks as well, like Bloody Marys. I love a good Bloody Mary. In my mind, it should be spicy and packed with garnishes, like a salad in a glass.

For the unfamiliar, passata is basically pureed tomatoes; you can find it in glass jars near the canned or crushed tomatoes in higher-end grocery stores or Italian markets. I like it because it's strained, and therefore a little thicker than canned tomatoes, so it's a nice place to start this drink, which will be thinned out with pickle juice. If you can't find it, simply substitute 3 cups tomato juice. If you're planning ahead, consider making a batch of infused vodka (page 149) for these—flavored with jalapeños, cucumber peels, or dill fronds. **SERVES 6 TO 8**

1. Mix together all of the ingredients, except the garnishes, in a pitcher, if you have one, or a large bowl if you don't.

2. Prepare glasses with ice and any desired garnishes, then divide the Bloody Marys among them. Serve immediately.

DILL PICKLE BRINE BLOODY MARY

1 jar (25 ounces) passata (see headnote)

½ cup dill pickle brine

¼ cup freshly squeezed lemon juice

1 teaspoon Worcestershire sauce

2 teaspoons prepared horseradish

¼ teaspoon celery seed

2 teaspoons (or more!) hot sauce
   (I tend to use Cholula or Tabasco
   in these, but use what you like)

¾ teaspoon fine-grain sea salt

¾ teaspoon freshly ground black pepper

1 teaspoon chopped fresh dill (optional)

1¼ cups vodka

Garnishes: celery stalks, olives, lemon
   wedges, dill pickles and/or other
   types of pickles—really anything that
   sounds good to you

DILL PICKLE BRINE POTATO SALAD

3 pounds baby potatoes,
  any large ones halved

⅓ cup chopped scallions

¼ cup dill pickle brine

¼ cup mayonnaise

1 tablespoon whole-grain mustard

2 teaspoons prepared horseradish

2 tablespoons chopped fresh dill

Fine-grain sea salt

Freshly ground black pepper

I spent far too many of my childhood years convinced that mayonnaise was gross, in part due to soggy, overdressed potato salads—and as a result, I was skeptical of potato salad, too. Luckily, I finally learned the error of my ways—on both accounts—and have made up for lost time with a newfound love of lightly dressed potato salads like this one, which is an amalgamation of many beloved recipes. I like this best with small, waxier potatoes, but if you want to go wild, you could try a mix of potato varieties—even sweet ones. **SERVES 6 TO 8**

1. Place the potatoes in a large pot and cover with salted water to a depth of 1 inch. Bring to a boil. The potatoes are ready when a knife slides in easily, but the very center should still feel just a touch firm. This could take between 8 and 15 minutes depending on the size of the potatoes. If your potatoes vary in size or type, fish the individual pieces out of the water to let cool as soon as they're ready.

2. Drain the potatoes and transfer them to a medium-size bowl. Add the scallions, then immediately drizzle the pickle brine over them. Let the potatoes cool slightly. As they cool, toss them in the bowl a couple of times to help distribute the pickle brine and encourage it to soak in.

3. Place the mayonnaise, mustard, horseradish, and dill in a small bowl along with a healthy pinch of salt and a few grinds of black pepper. Whisk to combine.

4. Once the potatoes have cooled, drizzle them with the dressing, toss to coat, and adjust the seasonings to taste.

5. Serve immediately or let the potato salad hang out, covered, in the fridge overnight to let the flavors meld even more. It will keep for 3 to 5 days in the refrigerator.

Prepping a pineapple produces a *lot* of waste, from its tough skin to its spiky crown to its fibrous core. I never thought about how much pineapple flavor I was discarding until I came across Food52er Laura B.'s recipe for iced tea, lightly spiced with cinnamon and ginger, but mostly flavored with pineapple scraps. Now I wouldn't dream of pitching them and regularly put them to good use in lemonade or infused water (page 148). Pineapples are one item that I would definitely recommend buying organic and (as with any produce!) scrubbing them really well before using the peel.

I like my lemonade mouth-puckeringly tart. If you do too, make a half-batch of the simple syrup (page 32), as you won't use very much of it. This makes a delicious nonalcoholic beverage, but if you're looking for something a little stronger, feel free to spike it—perhaps with strawberry-top vodka (page 148). **MAKES ABOUT 5 CUPS**

1. Place the pineapple core and pieces of peel in a medium-size pot, add 4 cups water, and bring to a boil over medium-high heat. Lower the heat and simmer, covered, for 25 minutes.

2. Remove the pot from the heat, add the mint sprigs, and let the mixture steep, covered, for 25 minutes.

3. Strain the mixture into a pitcher or serving vessel and discard the pineapple core, peel, and mint sprigs.

4. Add the lemon juice to the pineapple-infused water, stir, and slowly start adding simple syrup, tasting as you go, until the lemonade is sweetened to your liking.

5. Refrigerate until chilled. This lemonade is at its best the day it is made, but can be kept for a few days in the refrigerator. Stir before serving.

6. Any remaining simple syrup can be stored in an airtight container in the fridge for a couple of weeks.

NOTE: You'll have a lot of spent lemons! Use them in chicken stock (page 129) or for a lemon simple syrup (follow Step 2 of Whey Cool Limeade, page 169).

PINEAPPLE PEEL AND CORE LEMONADE WITH MINT

Peel and core from 1 pineapple
(see page 136)

3 generously sized mint sprigs

1 cup freshly squeezed lemon juice
(from 6 to 10 lemons—see Note)

1 cup simple syrup (page 32—if you need
to make a fresh batch, start it while
the pineapple is simmering in Step 1)

POTATOES

As many bread bakers know, a little potato can go a long way in a bread recipe—it can add moisture and help create a delicious, chewy crumb. Turns out the same can be said for potato peels and the starchy water left behind after cooking potatoes. Food52er Helen C. taught me to cook any leftover peels in water until tender, blitz the contents with an immersion blender, and save the mixture for use in rustic artisanal breads. If you're keeping the potato peels on the potatoes for your dish, simply use the cooking water alone. Potato peels can also be added to stock (see page 129), but note that they'll make it murky, so skip them when you're going for perfectly clear stock.

Much like Danish Pancakes (page 3), aebleskivers were a favorite childhood breakfast of mine. I'd treat the spherical puffy pancakes like finger food, popping them open and stuffing their bellies with butter, jam, cinnamon sugar, or some combination of the three.

Aebleskivers don't need to be confined to the sweet side of the spectrum, though; this recipe makes them savory with the inclusion of potato and chives. They do require a special pan (called . . . you guessed it, an aebleskiver pan), but you can make so many variations of them that it's worth it to pick one up if you haven't already. Serve them as an appetizer with sour cream for dipping, with a breakfast of eggs and bacon instead of toast, alongside hearty soups or stews, or anywhere you might want (adorably tiny) potato rolls. Try using dill or green onion tops instead of chives to slightly change up the flavor profile.

This recipe employs some of the water used to cook the potato, a trick that needn't be limited to aebleskivers. You can also put that slightly starchy water to good use in all of your favorite bread recipes. **SERVES 4 TO 6 AS A SIDE DISH**

POTATO WATER AND CHIVE AEBLE-SKIVERS

1 medium russet potato, chopped

½ teaspoon apple cider vinegar

1 cup whole milk (or 2%)

5 large eggs

¼ cup vegetable oil (or other neutral-flavored oil), plus more if necessary for the pan

2 cups all-purpose flour

1 teaspoon fine-grain sea salt

1 teaspoon baking soda

1 teaspoon baking powder

¼ cup finely chopped chives

1. Place the potato in a medium-size pan with water to cover. Bring the water to a boil over high heat, then lower to a simmer until the potato is fully cooked, about 15 minutes. Drain the water, reserving 1 cup. Mash the potato with a fork in a medium-size bowl and let cool slightly.

2. While the potato is cooking, stir the vinegar and milk together in a measuring cup or small bowl, and set aside for a few minutes to curdle.

3. Add the eggs to the bowl with the potato and whisk well. Add the oil, curdled milk, and potato water and whisk again to combine.

4. Place the flour, salt, baking soda, and baking powder in a large bowl, and whisk to combine. Add the egg mixture to the dry ingredients and whisk until just combined. Add the chives and whisk.

5. Heat your aebleskiver pan over medium heat and add a drop of oil into each well if necessary. (You'll learn your pan: I use two pans at the same time—one doesn't need oil and the other does. If you don't know, start with a drop of oil.) Add batter to fill each well three quarters of the way. The visual cues for aebleskivers are similar to those for pancakes: When they're ready to flip, after about 3 minutes, the edges will look set and the middle will still look raw, with bubbles coming up. I like to flip them with chopsticks. Use one chopstick to push down gently on a set edge, coaxing the aebleskiver to turn over with the other chopstick resting on the cooked side. Then let it finish cooking for another 2 to 3 minutes. If you've timed this well, you'll end up with a spherical pancake. If you flip it too late, there won't be enough raw batter to run down into the well of the pan and form the aebleskiver's other side—it will remain dome-shaped, but it will still taste good!

6. Serve immediately. I think they're best piping hot, so I like to serve them as they're done, but if you'd rather, you can put them in a baking dish in the oven at its lowest setting (likely 200°F or "warm") until you finish cooking the whole batch. If you have leftovers, store them in an airtight container in the freezer and reheat in a low oven until warmed through.

When you hear the word *pumpkin,* you might think of a large, round orange specimen ready for carving, but any sizeable hard-skinned squash could be called a pumpkin—there's no botanical distinction. (While I'm smashing pumpkin misconceptions, did you know that canned pumpkin purée is often made with other types of winter squash, like butternut?) Talk to your local farmers at the market about the best varieties for your dish, and whatever you make, remember to salvage the guts for another purpose. The seeds can be roasted (see page 145) and the fibrous webbing can be put to use, too, like in stock (see page 129) or baked goods (see page 143).

I started making these years ago when I was living in Japan and searching for baked goods that I could pull off in our teeny-tiny convection oven. Scones were an easy win. I loosely adapted Love and Olive Oil's Pumpkin Scones with Cinnamon Sugar Glaze to create sweet potato scones with butterscotch chips, and they remained in regular rotation—even after I got back to a standard oven. Then I modified them once again to make use of the webbing inside of a pumpkin—the guts, if you will.

After scraping out the insides of a sugar pie pumpkin (or cheese pumpkin, or other winter squash with a lot of innards), use your fingers to separate the seeds from the webbing (and save them for roasting, page 145). I call for ⅓ cup webbing, but if you have more, feel free to use up to ½ cup for especially moist scones.

Butterscotch chips do something special for these scones, but they can be hard to find. If you can't get your hands on them, it's fine to omit or to try white chocolate chips instead.

Plan ahead: This recipe works best when the ingredients are really cold, so at a couple of points you'll be putting bowls in the freezer—make some space before you get started. **MAKES 8 SCONES**

1. Preheat the oven to 425°F and line a baking sheet with parchment paper.

2. Melt 1 tablespoon of the butter in a small saucepan over medium heat, add the pumpkin webbing, and cook until it starts to soften and break down, about 5 minutes. Once it's cooked, I like to blitz it quickly with an immersion blender to get it really smooth. If you aren't burdened with perfectionist tendencies, mashing it with a fork would work just as well.

3. Meanwhile, cut the remaining 6 tablespoons of butter into small pieces, put the pieces into a small bowl, and set the bowl in the freezer.

4. Whisk together the flour, baking powder, salt, cinnamon, nutmeg, and ginger in a medium-size bowl. Set the bowl in the freezer.

PUMPKIN GUTS BUTTERSCOTCH SCONES

7 tablespoons unsalted butter

⅓ cup pumpkin webbing, lightly packed

2 cups all-purpose flour, plus more for flouring the work surface

1½ teaspoons baking powder

½ teaspoon fine-grain sea salt

½ teaspoon ground cinnamon

¼ teaspoon ground nutmeg

½ teaspoon ground ginger

⅓ cup heavy whipping cream

⅓ cup lightly packed light or dark brown sugar

1 teaspoon vanilla extract

¼ cup butterscotch chips

¼ cup roasted pumpkin seeds (optional—follow the instructions for Everything Bagel Roasted Pumpkin Seeds, page 145, use only salt, pumpkin seeds, and oil)

5. Place the softened pumpkin, cream, brown sugar, and vanilla extract in another small bowl and whisk to combine. Set this bowl in the freezer and remove the bowls with the butter and the flour mixture.

6. Cut the butter into the flour mixture with a pastry cutter (or two knives) until the mixture looks like coarse crumbs and you still have small pieces of butter visible.

7. Remove the pumpkin mixture from the freezer and gently fold it into the flour and butter mixture. Then stir in the butterscotch chips.

8. Form the dough into a circle on a lightly floured surface, pat it to about 1 inch thick, then slice it into 8 wedges. Sprinkle the roasted pumpkin seeds on top, if using.

9. Put the scones on the baking sheet, and bake until they are light brown on the bottom, about 15 minutes. After cooling on a baking rack, serve warm or at room temperature. Although they rarely make it past the first day in my household, the scones can be stored in an airtight container or zip-top bag at room temperature for a couple days.

As I mentioned with cantaloupe seeds (page 118), the seeds of all members of the Cucurbitaceae family are edible, so you can try roasting the seeds of all types of winter squash. Note that smaller squash like butternut will have smaller and fewer seeds, so they'll roast more quickly, and might not need all of the spice blend—save some for a future batch!

Some people swear that boiling the seeds for 10 minutes or so before roasting improves their texture. I've never found that it made that much of a difference—not enough to bother with washing an extra pot anyway—but if you do, by all means, do that step first. In that vein, I often skip the bowl in Step 2 and toss everything together right on the baking sheet—again, the fewer dishes, the better.

The best part of carving pumpkins? Roasting the seeds, of course. The best bagel flavor? Everything! And the two combined? Just as good as you'd imagine. **MAKES 1 BATCH OF SEEDS FOR SHARING (OR SAVING)**

1. Preheat the oven to 375°F.

2. Mix the sesame seeds, poppy seeds, minced onion, garlic powder, smoked paprika, and sea salt together in a small bowl.

3. Place the pumpkin seeds in a medium-size bowl, drizzle with the olive oil, toss to coat, then add the spice mixture and toss again.

4. Spread the seeds out on a baking sheet in a single layer and roast until golden brown, 10 to 20 minutes. Don't worry if they aren't crunchy right out of the oven. Let them cool on the baking sheet—they will crisp up more as they cool. The seeds can be stored in an airtight container or zip-top bag at room temperature.

EVERY-THING BAGEL ROASTED PUMPKIN SEEDS

1 tablespoon sesame seeds

1½ teaspoons poppy seeds

1 tablespoon dried minced onion

1 teaspoon garlic powder

¼ teaspoon smoked paprika

1 teaspoon fine-grain sea salt

Seeds from 1 large pumpkin, rinsed and dried

1 tablespoon extra virgin olive oil

Radishes are one of the earliest delights of spring. They're like a ray of sunshine at the market, bringing a much-needed pop of color even as the weather continues to waffle back and forth (at least in my neck of the woods), consoling us that warmth is surely right around the corner. Chop up the radish tops and add them to a salad (whether green, grain, potato, or egg), sauté them and sprinkle them over any dish that would benefit from a bit of a bite, or turn them into a side dish in their own right (page 147).

O*hitashi* is a common method of treating vegetables in Japan—most often spinach. *Hitashi* is a verb meaning "to soak" (the *o* is simply an honorific prefix), so as you might be able to guess, this means the vegetables are soaked in a flavorful blend of dashi, mirin, and soy sauce. I generally eat this as a vegetable side dish, but it also makes a nice addition to a rice bowl with other toppings. **SERVES 1 OR 2 AS A SMALL SIDE DISH**

1. Fill a medium-size pot with water and bring to a boil over high heat. Prepare an ice bath by filling a medium-size bowl with ice and water.

2. Mix together the dashi, mirin, and soy sauce in a small container—ideally one with a lid.

3. Blanch the greens for 1 minute in the boiling water and then transfer them to the ice bath to stop the cooking.

4. When the greens are cool enough to touch, squeeze the water out of them, chop them into bite-size pieces, and add them to the container with the dashi mixture.

5. Refrigerate for at least 1 hour and serve—with or without the soaking liquid—with toasted sesame seeds sprinkled on top.

RADISH TOP OHITASHI

½ cup dashi or kelp stock, or ¼ cup lightly flavored vegetable broth and ¼ cup water (see box)

1 tablespoon mirin

2 teaspoons soy sauce

Greens from 1 bunch radishes

1 tablespoon toasted sesame seeds, for garnish (see page 22)

Kelp stock is made by soaking dried kelp, also known as *kombu*, in water. Dashi starts the same way, but includes bonito flakes—dried flakes of fish that have been smoked and fermented. Dashi is very mild in flavor, so if substituting vegetable broth, use only half as much and make up the difference with water. You'll be able to find these ingredients at a well-stocked grocery store, health food store, an Asian market, or online.

Infused Alcohols.

I wasn't introduced to the writing of novelist and columnist for *Gourmet* magazine Laurie Colwin until decades after her untimely death, and I flew through her books, all the while desperately wishing she were still alive and writing. Her voice was comforting and familiar, and I felt myself agreeing with her at every turn, often with an excessive number of mental exclamation points. I felt like I'd found a new friend in her words.

I challenged myself to make all of the gingerbread cakes she wrote about (five, if you're curious, due to a couple of variations and a nutmeg cake that I decided to count), and I came away with a new appreciation for gingerbread and a love for infusing alcohol. In *Home Cooking*, one cake calls for both lemon brandy (made by steeping strips of zest from two lemons in four ounces of brandy) and vanilla brandy (same concept as the lemon brandy, but with vanilla pods instead of lemon zest). Long after the cake was consumed, I found

myself continuing to make batches of vanilla brandy and experimenting with other types of alcoholic infusions, too.

I've included three of my favorites on page 150, but don't stop there. If you're hulling pints of strawberries, and your berry tops still have slivers of red fruit attached, drop those tops into some medium-quality vodka to make **strawberry top vodka**. If you're shucking ears of corn, keep the papery husks, spread them out on a baking sheet, and toast them in a 300°F oven until lightly browned and golden, 20 to 25 minutes. Use the **cooled husks** to infuse **bourbon**. Play around and make

coriander, carrot, and dill gin

vanilla pod bourbon

blood orange, ginger, and lemongrass water

serrano tequila

different combinations, taste them regularly, and once the infusion is as flavorful as you'd like, strain it to remove the scrap and return the liquor to a clear jar or other container.

With whatever infusion you make, good straining is key. High-proof alcohols keep pretty much indefinitely, but if any little bits of your infusion agent get left behind, they can start to degrade and change the flavor. Your infusions should be fine in the pantry for months, but use common sense and toss them if they start to smell or taste off. Of course, the hope is that they won't last *that*

Scraps can be used to infuse water, too: strawberry tops (add a sprig of mint if you have it), fruit peels that you don't want to turn into sugar (page 85), cucumber peels and ends, extra herbs, spent citrus halves, pits from stone fruit that still have fruit clinging to them (from slicing around them, not chewing on them!), and more.

long because you'll be inspired to use them up in your favorite cocktails.

You might have realized by now that margaritas are one of my favorites. While the Beet Peel Margarita (page 32) is fitting for

cooler weather, the recipe that follows is just right for hot summer days. Add a little cilantro when you muddle the blueberries, or swap in other fruit depending on what's in season, like strawberries or pineapple. And if you have

cucumber
lemon
water

pineapple
tarragon
water

beet
vodka

thyme
bourbon

orange and
mint water

leftover lime simple syrup from making Whey Cool Limeade (page 169), by all means use it.

BLUEBERRY JALAPEÑO MARGARITA

MAKES 2 COCKTAILS (SHARING IS OPTIONAL)

Kosher salt

Small handful of blueberries (about ¼ cup)

1 ounce Cointreau or other orange-flavored liqueur

2 limes, juiced (don't discard the spent limes)

3 ounces Jalapeño Tequila (recipe follows)

4 teaspoons simple syrup (see page 32)

1. Pour some kosher salt into a small dish.

2. Muddle the blueberries in the bottom of a cocktail shaker, then add the Cointreau, lime juice, tequila, simple syrup, and ice to fill.

3. Run the spent lime halves around the rims of two glasses (or one, no judgment), dip the rims in the salt, and then fill the glasses with ice.

4. Shake the cocktail until chilled, then strain into the two glasses.

VANILLA POD BRANDY

MAKES AT LEAST 4 OUNCES

Scraped vanilla pods, seeds used for another purpose

Brandy (see Step 2 to determine quantity)

1. Cut up the vanilla pod so the pieces fit flat in the bottom of the container you're using. I like to use a 1½-pint Ball jar so I can continue to add to it over time.

2. For every 1 spent pod, add 4 ounces of brandy.

3. Allow to sit and steep for 2 weeks before using. Store the sealed container in a cool, dark place.

4. Continue to add more spent pods to the container and top off with more brandy as you use it. It will keep at least 3 weeks, possibly longer.

BEET PEEL TEQUILA

MAKES AT LEAST 4 OUNCES

Peels from 2 raw beets, cut off in wide strips

Gold tequila (see Step 1 to determine quantity)

1. Loosely pack the beet peel pieces in a glass jar with an airtight lid, and pour tequila over them until just covered; you'll probably need about 4 ounces.

2. Allow the mixture to sit and steep for 10 days. Strain the tequila, discard the beet peels, then return the tequila to a clean, sealable container, and store it in a cool, dark place for up to 3 weeks.

JALAPEÑO TEQUILA

MAKES ABOUT 4 OUNCES

Tops and ribs from jalapeño or serrano peppers (seeds are optional; they don't add anything, but there's no need to remove them either)

Gold tequila (see Step 1 to determine quantity)

1. Place the jalapeño scraps in a glass jar with an airtight lid and pour tequila over them until just covered; for 2 or 3 peppers you'll probably need at least 4 ounces.

2. Let steep for 1 to 3 days, tasting daily! Do not forget about this infusion; it can become too spicy if you're not careful. Strain the tequila, discard the pepper parts, return the tequila to a clean, sealable container, and store it in a cool, dark place for up to 3 weeks.

NOTE: The spiciest part of a pepper is the ribs, so if you want to tone down the kick, stick with just the tops.

The pits of stone fruits—such as peaches and plums—are one kitchen scrap that's easy to toss in the compost bin without remorse. But inside of those pits are the stone fruits' seeds (also called kernels). And those are, in fact, useful—very useful. They can be added to jams; substituted for some of the almonds in cookies and biscotti; and used as a flavoring agent in liqueurs, simple syrups, vinegars, and desserts like crème anglaise.

STONE FRUIT PIT LIQUEUR

1 cup stone fruit pits
(peaches, nectarines, plums,
and apricots—see headnote)

1 cup vodka

½ cup simple syrup (page 32),
or to taste

Crème de Noyaux (or Liqueur de Noyaux)—the inspiration for this recipe—is a liqueur flavored with apricot kernels, as are some brands of amaretto. The French word *noyaux* refers to the seeds, or kernels, inside of stone fruit pits.

Cooking with and eating apricot kernels makes some people nervous, as they contain a small amount of cyanide, and it's true that a small handful of raw kernels could cause a stomachache, or worse, but making this liqueur shouldn't give you pause. For one thing, I incorporate chef Alice Waters's method of double-roasting the kernels, which reduces or eliminates the harmful substance. For another, this version uses a mix of stone fruit pits, not just apricots—I keep my blend to one-third or less apricot pits. And finally, in all likelihood, you aren't consuming the entire finished liqueur in one sitting. **MAKES ABOUT 8 OUNCES**

1. Preheat the oven to 350°F.

2. Roast the pits on a baking sheet for 10 minutes, then remove from the oven. Leave the oven on, but let the pits cool enough to touch. Wrap them in an old, clean tea towel (not your favorite one, as it might get a little beat up), set them on a sturdy cutting board, and whack them with a hammer to crack open the pits. It's okay if some kernels get smashed in the process, and it's not necessary to hit them really hard; just persistently tap until they give way. If you're having trouble, try holding each pit in place with a pair of pliers.

Unless you're making a peach pie, you might not have a cup of pits on hand—simply collect pits in an airtight container or zip-top bag in the freezer until you get enough. If you're starting with frozen pits, increase the initial baking time to 15 minutes.

3. Place the kernels on the baking sheet again, and return them to the oven for 5 minutes. Remove and let them cool slightly.

4. Combine the roasted kernels and the vodka in a sealable container and let sit for 1 month.

5. After a month, strain the resulting liqueur through a cheesecloth-lined strainer and mix with simple syrup to taste. Return to a clean, sealed container and store in a cool, dark place. High-proof alcohols have a long shelf life, but plan for a 3-month lifespan (though it could last longer).

TOMATOES

Every afternoon in the summertime, my daughter and I walk back to collect a small handful of ripe yellow pear tomatoes from our garden. She'll neatly bite the very top off of one, suck out its insides, and say, "Mmm. I needed a tomato drink, Mama!" Most of the time, she'll then eat the rest of the tomato, but every so often she hands the shell of the tomato to me for polishing off—she's deemed the seeds and tomato water the best part. Smart kid (who's biased? me?)—she's already learned how flavorful the insides of tomatoes are, yet all too often we discard them. Whether we're draining slices for a BLT or tomato pie, that tomato water is left to run off cutting boards and pool on countertops, awaiting its fate of being swiped up into a sponge or paper towel. Make a pact with yourself to not waste another drop of tomato water—or tomato peels or unripe tomatoes either, for that matter.

Really juicy tomatoes are a highlight of summer, but sometimes they're *so* juicy that there's too much liquid for your dish—no one wants a soggy tomato sandwich! But don't toss the pulpy seeds and tomato liquid—they are too flavorful to be discarded. Make this dressing instead. **MAKES A SCANT ⅔ CUP**

1. Process the tomato seeds and juice, miso, lemon juice, olive oil, and basil in a food processor until well blended.

2. Taste and add salt if necessary, and process again.

3. The dressing can be stored in an airtight container in the refrigerator for 2 to 3 days, but the flavor of the lemon juice starts to degrade after a day—it's best the day it is made.

BASIL–TOMATO SEED DRESSING

¼ cup tomato innards, including the seeds and any liquid

1 teaspoon white miso paste

1½ tablespoons freshly squeezed lemon juice

¼ cup extra virgin olive oil

½ cup basil leaves, torn or chopped

Fine-grain sea salt

BLACK BEAN AND GREEN TOMATO PICO DE GALLO

2 cans (15 ounces each) black beans, drained and rinsed (see box)

3 cups diced green tomatoes (from 5 or 6 medium-size tomatoes)

1 medium-size white onion, diced (about 1 cup)

½ cup sliced green olives

2 red or green serrano peppers, seeded and minced

2 or 3 garlic cloves, minced

1 cup chopped cilantro

2 teaspoons fine-grain sea salt

½ cup freshly squeezed lime juice

Tortilla chips, for serving (optional)

I f you have your own garden, the end of summer almost inevitably brings with it a bounty of green tomatoes that never have a chance to get ripe (maybe this doesn't happen in more southern states; don't tell me if that's the case). I love fried green tomatoes, but there's a limit to how often I can make them. When I lamented my overload of green tomatoes to my friend Brittany Zeller-Holland, she mentioned that she was using hers for salsa, and I was inspired to make a riff on one of my favorite black bean salsa recipes. As written, this has a pico de gallo consistency, but I also like it as a salsa—blitz the tomatoes with an immersion blender or in a regular blender before mixing in the other ingredients.

If you don't have a garden, visit your local farmers market and you'll almost certainly be able to find green tomatoes at the end of the season. Change up this recipe with a red onion or a generous bunch or two of green onions instead of the white onion; add some corn stripped off the cob; or use black olives instead of green. **MAKES ABOUT 8 CUPS**

1. Combine the black beans, green tomatoes, onion, green olives, serranos, garlic, cilantro, salt, and lime juice in a medium-size bowl. Adjust seasoning to taste—it might need a little more lime juice or salt.

2. The pico de gallo can be eaten with tortilla chips immediately, but it's best when refrigerated, covered, for an hour or two, or even overnight, to allow the flavors to mingle.

Keep the leftover bean liquid and make Fudgy Aquafaba Brownies (page 9).

TURNIPS

Envision a turnip and you are not picturing a sexy vegetable. Your lips aren't curling up at the edges like they might when you think of purple asparagus, pea shoots, or the season's first punnets of strawberries. But I'd argue this is because you are thinking of January turnips: the storage crops that one might diligently add to mashes and stews in a devotion to seasonal eating. The truth is: They can be tough, stringy, and bitter. Let's be honest, though… don't we all get a little bitter in the depths of winter? Spring turnips are like another vegetable altogether—they're small, creamy white, and crisp, with just the right amount of bite. Plus, unlike winter turnips, spring turnips offer a free gift with purchase: their greens. Young turnip tops tend to be sweeter and can be tossed in a salad, but you'll likely want to cook them. Use the greens in comforting staples, like beans, gratins, soups, and stews, or turn them into a pesto.

Miso soup is generally made with a base of dashi—broth made from steeping kombu and bonito flakes, often overnight. This miso soup is a quickie version and, while it isn't traditional, it's very tasty all the same. If you're inclined to use the whole turnip instead of just the greens, thinly slice or grate the raw root and use it to garnish the top of the finished dish. **SERVES 4**

1. Place the sesame oil in a medium-size pot over medium heat. Once the oil has warmed up, add the ginger, garlic, white parts of the green onions, and the chopped turnip stems. Sauté, stirring occasionally, until the white parts of the green onions are nearly translucent and the turnip stem pieces are tender, 5 to 7 minutes.

2. Add the broth to the pot and raise the heat to medium-high. Once the broth is very hot, but not boiling, place the miso in a small bowl, whisk in about 1 cup of the hot broth to make a slurry, then add that mixture back to the pot. Turn off the heat, but leave the pot on the burner, and add the green parts of the green onions, shredded turnip greens, and tofu. Let it stand for a moment to heat everything through and wilt the greens, then serve immediately.

Stop peeling your ginger! The most tender, flavorful part of the rhizome is right under the skin, and there's really no need to peel ginger, for this recipe or any other (okay, unless it looks extremely dried out or there's dirt hiding between the fingers that is impossible to scrub out with a vegetable brush).

GINGER-GARLIC MISO SOUP WITH TURNIP GREENS

2 tablespoons untoasted sesame oil (or another neutral-flavored oil)

2 tablespoons very finely minced or grated fresh ginger (see box)

1 or 2 garlic cloves, very finely minced

5 or 6 green onions, white and green parts separated, each finely chopped

1 small bunch turnip greens, stems and central ribs removed and finely chopped, leaves shredded or left whole if small

5 cups mild-flavored low-sodium vegetable broth (or water—the soup will have plenty of flavor)

¼ cup white miso paste

4 to 8 ounces firm tofu, cubed

COCONUT MILK–BRAISED TURNIP GREENS STEW

1 tablespoon unsalted butter

1 tablespoon coconut oil

1 small white or yellow onion, chopped

1 bunch turnip greens (see Note), stems finely chopped and leaves roughly chopped or in 1/4-inch chiffonade (see page 34)

1 garlic clove, minced

1 medium-size Yukon Gold potato, grated

1 cup coconut milk

1 cup vegetable stock, either store-bought or homemade (page 129)

Freshly ground black pepper

1 teaspoon apple cider vinegar

Fine-grain sea salt

Longtime Food52er Jennifer Perillo has a recipe for milk-braised beet greens, in which she thickens the dish with a grated fingerling potato. It's a great trick to apply in many situations, and I use it in this dish, which is inspired by hers, but with a larger, less waxy potato to give it even more heft. This rather simple stew comes together quickly and is comforting on a cool night with just a hunk of crusty bread. **SERVES 2**

1. Add the butter and coconut oil to a medium-size pot over medium heat. Once the butter and oil have melted, add the onion and chopped stems and cook until the onion is translucent and softened, 5 to 7 minutes. Add the garlic and cook until fragrant, 1 minute or less.

2. Add the turnip greens, potato, coconut milk, vegetable stock, and a few grinds of pepper to the pot, lower the heat to medium-low, and simmer, partially covered, until the potato softens and the stew thickens up, about 15 minutes.

3. Add the apple cider vinegar and taste to adjust for salt—the amount will depend on how salty your stock was. Serve immediately.

NOTE: If you happen to need to use a leftover turnip or two (or more), dice them and add them in with the onions in Step 1.

VANILLA

For an intense, pure vanilla flavor, nothing beats fresh vanilla pods. I love splitting them open, scraping out the seeds, and watching them freckle whatever I'm making. And it's not just the seeds that are packed with vanilla flavor. The pods are, too, and will lend their vanilla essence to everything from homemade vanilla extract and vanilla sugar to infused liquor (see page 148) and cream (see Fennel Stalk Ice Cream with Lemon and Vanilla Bean, page 94).

VANILLA POD BRANDY HOT TODDY

1 tea bag (there's no wrong choice here, use one that sounds good to you—choose one without caffeine, like chamomile, if you're drinking this before bed; caffeinated, like black tea, works, too)

½ to 1 teaspoon honey, or to taste

Peppermint candy (the round red and white kind, or a mini candy cane)

1 ounce Vanilla Pod Brandy (page 150)

1 lemon wedge

One of my dads, Greg, has a culinary specialty that is a bit unusual: tea. Yes, tea. No, it's not hard to make a cup of tea, but his is always the best. It starts with a random tea bag plucked from a jumbled collection in a large Ball jar, hot water of course, a wedge of lemon, and then the pièce de résistance—a double shot of sweetness from honey and a peppermint candy. And if you're feeling a little under the weather, he'll add a splash of bourbon. Even though I know how he makes it, mine never comes out quite as good, but I keep trying anyway. This is my ode to his cuppa. **SERVES 1**

1. Bring water to a boil in a teakettle.

2. Place the tea bag in a large mug along with a squeeze of honey and the peppermint candy. Pour in the hot water leaving a little space at the top. Let the tea steep for a moment or two.

3. Pour in the brandy, squeeze in the lemon, and give it a stir. The honey will dissolve; it's okay if the peppermint candy doesn't fully. Serve while the tea is still steaming hot.

VANILLA POD EXTRACT

Homemade vanilla extract and vanilla sugar are most commonly made with whole vanilla beans, but they work just as well with split and scraped vanilla pods. Why not use those flavorful seeds elsewhere and get the best of both worlds? **MAKES 1 CUP**

4 spent vanilla pods (split and scraped, seeds used elsewhere)

1 cup mid-range vodka (see box)

1. Choose an airtight container (like a glass jar) and cut the vanilla pods into shorter lengths so that they fit in the jar and will be covered by the vodka. Add them to the container.

2. Pour the vodka into the container, close it, and keep in a cool, dark place for at least two months, ideally three. At that point, your extract is ready to use. Since you typically use so little at a time, it's fine to top it off with more vodka as needed, and keep adding spent pods to it as well. Vanilla extract keeps indefinitely, but it might lose flavor if exposed to heat or light, so store it in a cool, dark place.

Vodka is most commonly used to make extract, but other types of liquor work, too! Try using rum, brandy, bourbon, or even tequila to get slightly different results.

VANILLA POD SUGAR

It's amazing how much flavor spent vanilla pods can still provide, especially in sugar. Use vanilla sugar as you would regular granulated sugar, anywhere you'd like an additional touch of vanilla flavor. It's so good, you'll start looking for excuses to use it. **MAKES 1 CUP**

2 spent vanilla pods (split and scraped, seeds used elsewhere)

1 cup granulated sugar

1. Choose an airtight container (like a glass jar) and cut the vanilla pods into shorter lengths to fit inside. Add them to the container.

2. Add the sugar to the container, close it, and shake to combine. Keep the container in a cool, dry place for two weeks to allow the vanilla flavor to infuse the sugar. Stored in an airtight container, vanilla sugar will last indefinitely.

Whey is the liquid that remains after making cheese (see Peanut Shell–Infused Pot Cheese, page 125). If you're making your own cheese at home (and you should—it will make you feel like a kitchen magician), you should be saving the whey. It has a subtle sweetness and is said to give breads and other baked goods a softer crumb. I store it in the freezer in an airtight, freezer-safe container until I'm ready to use it. Then I put it to work to cook rice or grits, to replace the water in a bread recipe, or as an ingredient in one of the following two recipes.

Red lentil soup is one of the easiest soups to make—it comes together quickly, but is thick and comforting. Whey gives it a creamy element that water or broth alone won't. Don't worry about waiting to accumulate 4 cups of whey. You can play around with the ratio of whey to water—the goal is to have 6 cups of liquid. If you have only a cup or two of whey, you can supplement it with vegetable or chicken stock to boost the flavor, as this is a mild-flavored soup to begin with.

The finished soup is just as calming in color as it is in flavor. I like to accent its pale hue—whether it turns out a shade of yellow or a pinkish-orange—with just a sprinkle of tangy sumac, but you could also add a sprinkle of chopped fresh parsley if you'd like to liven it up further. **SERVES 4 TO 6**

1. Place the red lentils, onion, whey, and 2 cups water in a large pot and bring to a boil over medium-high heat. Reduce the heat to medium, and simmer, covered, until the onion is very tender and the lentils are essentially mush, 25 to 35 minutes.

2. Stir in the salt, cumin, and juice from 1 lemon, then adjust the seasonings to taste, adding more salt and lemon juice if needed.

3. Sprinkle a pinch of sumac, if using, on each serving for an additional boost of flavor (and visual interest). Serve hot. The soup can be stored in an airtight container in the refrigerator.

RED LENTIL AND WHEY SOUP

2 cups red lentils (whole or split), rinsed and picked over

1 medium-size onion, diced (about 1 cup)

4 cups whey

1 teaspoon fine-grain sea salt

1 teaspoon ground cumin

Juice from 1 or 2 lemons

Ground sumac, for garnish (optional)

S arah Jampel, one of my former colleagues at Food52, introduced me to the idea of lacto-fermented lemonade. Although the word *fermented* may conjure up images of intensely flavored foods (like kimchi), that's not the case with lacto-fermented lemonade—or limeade in this case; it's actually pretty mellow and ever-so-slightly creamy. Since it isn't quite as pucker-inducing tart as traditional limeade, I wanted to maximize the full flavor of the citrus by drawing out the rest of the flavor from the juiced lime peels in a simple syrup.

Be patient, you won't be drinking this limeade today—as this is a fermented beverage, it takes time, so plan ahead. You'll probably have extra syrup. Use it in other beverages, like a Beet Peel Margarita (page 32). It will keep in the refrigerator for up to 2 weeks. **MAKES ABOUT ½ GALLON**

1. Squeeze the limes into a half-gallon (8-cup) container with a lid (don't discard the spent limes!) and add the whey and ½ cup of the sugar. Add water to fill up the container to about 1 inch from the top, stir, and put the lid on. Leave the container at room temperature for 2 to 5 days.

2. Take the spent limes and cut each half in half again. Put them in a small bowl with the remaining ¾ cup sugar. Stir them together and let the mixture sit—either on the counter or in the fridge—for at least 6 hours and up to 12 hours. Stir occasionally as the mixture sits, then remove the limes after the time is up. You're left with a super limey-sugary syrup. The sugar probably won't have dissolved completely. If that's the case, heat the syrup in a small pot over medium heat until it dissolves. Then, transfer the (cooled) mixture to a glass jar or similar container and refrigerate until ready to use.

3. Once you're happy with how your whey limeade base tastes, add in some of the lime syrup. Start with a tablespoon or two, taste as you go, and refrigerate it once you're satisfied with the level of sweetness.

4 You can serve this in glasses over ice, straight up, or mixed with sparkling water, especially one with a subtle complementary flavor (my favorite is coconut LaCroix).

WHEY COOL LIMEADE

1 pound limes (about 5), halved

½ cup whey

1¼ cups granulated sugar

Ice and/or sparkling water (see Step 4), for serving (optional)

Infused Vinegars.

It couldn't be easier to make your own flavored versions of this pantry staple: Take your flavoring agent, place it in a jar, cover with vinegar (my default is white wine vinegar), and let them hang out until the vinegar is properly infused (check this by tasting it; some blends might need only one week, others might need three). Strain the vinegar, transfer it to a clean glass container with a lid, and store in a cupboard or other cool, dark place. Vinegar has an indefinite shelf life, but since it's possible everything might not get strained out of yours, plan for a three-month lifespan (though it could last longer). Flavored vinegars are lovely in vinaigrettes or sprinkled on any dish that could use livening up.

HERB SCRAP VINEGAR

Make herb-infused vinegars with lingering herbs on their last legs or the stems from woody herbs like thyme or rosemary. I tend to stick to one herb at a time, but feel free to go crazy and make your own herb blends.

FRUIT SCRAP VINEGAR

Try making fruity vinegars with your fruit scraps: strawberry tops in champagne vinegar, orange peels in apple cider vinegar, little nubs of ginger in either.

For more of a specific recipe, try Chive Blossom Vinegar. I was introduced to this vinegar thanks to Marisa McClellan's blog, Food in Jars. My love for this vinegar necessitated the addition of chives to my garden, so I'd always have a supply of blossoms. If you

don't grow your own, pick up an extra bunch at the farmers market—you'll want enough to make some vinegar for yourself and some to give as gifts.

CHIVE BLOSSOM VINEGAR

MAKES 1 JAR

Chive blossoms (at least 1 medium-size bundle, but I like to put in as many as I can get my hands on)

White wine vinegar or other light-colored vinegar, like distilled or champagne vinegar (see Step 2)

1. Put your chive blossoms in a jar. Pick a container that you can fill at least halfway with blossoms —I go even farther and fill mine two-thirds to three-quarters full of blossoms. Use a container with a wide enough neck that the blossoms will easily come back out—I

use glass canning jars, from half-pint up to quart-size, depending on how many blossoms I have.

2. Fill your jar with vinegar. You want to stick with a clear or light-colored vinegar, so you don't miss out on the delicate purple color the blossoms will impart. You can use either a single type of vinegar or a blend. I generally do a mix of part white wine vinegar and part distilled vinegar, but I'm also partial to a blend of mostly distilled vinegar with a small amount of ume plum vinegar.

3. Let your jar hang out in a cupboard (or other cool, dry place) for a week or two (stick to two weeks if your jar is only half full of blossoms), then strain the vinegar, discard the blossoms, and transfer the vinegar to a new jar.

One of my brothers, James (but Jimmy to me), lived in Paris for a little less than a year, and our whole family was lucky enough to make (separate) trips to visit him. I learned to stir a dollop of crème fraîche into pasta sauce, the joy of a simple meal with quality ingredients (baguette, cheese, and hummus, all procured from nearby shops), and the beauty of having a "house wine"—a self-selected go-to bottle that you always have on hand. In Jimmy's case, Château Landrieu Bordeaux. My parents brought home a couple of bottles, one of which sat neglected in the basement for more than a decade—it was not designed to age for that long. It was no longer fit to drink, so my parents were all too happy to give it to me. They might not have, had they known that the wine was already well on its way to becoming a delicious batch of red wine vinegar.

T o make your own wine vinegar, there's no need to use old wine, and you don't need to start with a whole bottle. Any leftover wine will do — red, white, or sparkling (don't mix them; start separate batches of vinegar for each type you want to make). You don't need to add anything to your wine — time will turn it into vinegar all on its own — but that method is hit-or-miss. Sometimes it works like a charm, but other times you'll get moldy wine instead of wine vinegar. After seeing multiple friends' batches fail, I've come to the conclusion that it's easiest to give your vinegar a kickstart, either by purchasing a mother from a store or website that sells beer- and wine-making supplies or by mixing in some live vinegar, like Bragg Organic Raw Apple Cider Vinegar.

Once you've started making vinegars, you'll create your own mother that you can use for future batches, and I can almost guarantee that there will be more batches. Making your own vinegar is easy, and addictive, because the results are almost always better than what you can buy at the store. **QUANTITY DEPENDS ON HOW MUCH WINE YOU START WITH**

1. Measure the wine and pour it into a wide-mouth glass or ceramic jar or bowl. Add ⅓ cup live vinegar to the vessel for every 1 cup wine. Cover the container with a double layer of cheesecloth (to maintain airflow while keeping bugs out), secure it with a rubber band, and leave it in an out-of-the-way, room-temperature place.

2. After a week or two, you'll notice a skin or film forming on the surface. That's the mother, and it shouldn't be disturbed. You'll want to taste the mixture every so often to see how the process is going. (Do so by gently nudging the mother aside with your tasting spoon or a chopstick, taking care not to jostle it so much that it sinks to the bottom, or you'll start the waiting process all over again.) If you started with the equivalent of a glass or two, you can start checking around

WINE VINEGAR

Wine (see Note, page 174)

Live vinegar, like Bragg Organic Raw Apple Cider Vinegar

the 3-week mark. If you started with a full bottle, wait until at least a month and a half have passed. Keep tasting until it tastes like vinegar, and don't give up—it could take 2 or 3 months.

3. Once the mixture tastes nice and tart, discard the mother (or transfer it to a fresh jar to make a new batch of vinegar with more leftover wine), and store the vinegar in jars with airtight lids. (Exposure to air is essential for the fermentation part, but is no longer a good thing once your wine has turned into vinegar.) Store it in a cool, dark place. Vinegar has an indefinite shelf life and will probably taste even better after it has aged.

NOTE: Wine's alcohol content is typically in the 9 to 12 percent range, which just happens to be ideal for vinegar making. If you're using one that's higher than this range, say 15 percent or more, consider adding a little water to it, as too much alcohol can inhibit bacterial activity. (Don't stress out about this step: There's no need to measure it, a splash of water will do. And even if the alcohol content is still on the high side, your wine will turn into vinegar eventually; it just might take a little longer.)

Don't use corked wine to make vinegar! You want to use good wine that you like drinking. The wine I mentioned in the headnote was no longer good to drink, but it still smelled good, like a mix of wine and vinegar. If the wine smells bad, don't use it; the resulting vinegar won't taste good, either.

When zucchini and summer squash are young, they can be grated or sliced whole—skin, flesh, and seeds—for use in breads or refreshing salads, leaving behind only the stems. As I learned from chef Gabrielle Hamilton's cookbook, *Prune,* the stems are perfectly edible, too! (More on that in the following recipe.) As the season wears on, and the squash grow, the seeds have grown in size, too, and are ripe for roasting (follow the same strategy described on page 145). Squash blossoms are hardly a scrap and more of a treat if you can get your hands on them. The flower's reproductive parts inside the blossoms are edible, as is the calyx, the green leaf-like base—though some people prefer to remove the crunchy non-petal parts. Use the blossoms the day you get them. Slice them into ribbons and use them raw in salads. Wilt them in soups, sauté them for egg dishes, batter and fry them, or use them as a pizza topping.

When making pizza at home, I gravitate toward pizzas without tomato sauce, because unless you're cooking for a crowd, you need to make a very small batch of sauce or figure out how to use the leftovers. For this one, you'll use the garlic-infused oil that you cook the vegetables in.

As noted on the Beet Greens and Eggplant Pizza (page 30), if you're making your own dough (I'm fond of Roberta's and Jim Lahey's recipes—see page 30 for more on those), you can stick with a smaller 8-ounce ball. However, if you're buying premade dough at the store, I think it's easiest to use a larger amount. Premade dough is convenient, but doesn't seem to stretch out as well. **MAKES ONE 12-INCH PIZZA**

1. Preheat the oven to its highest bake setting, 500° or 550°F. Set a pizza stone or baking steel, if you have one, on the rack to preheat it.

2. Heat the oil in a large sauté pan over medium heat, add the garlic, and cook briefly until slightly softened and fragrant, 30 seconds to 1 minute.

3. Add the zucchini stems to the pan and cook until softened—if your pan is running hot, slightly charred spots are okay—about a minute.

4. Scooch the zucchini off to one side of the pan, then add the corn and cook until slightly softened, about 2 minutes—again, slightly charred spots are fine! Turn off the stovetop and shift the pan to a cool (unlit) burner.

5. Stretch the dough out into a roughly 12-inch circle. (See Step 4 on page 31 for more specific instructions on rolling out the dough.) Carefully remove the preheated pizza stone from the oven. Lightly sprinkle it with cornmeal and transfer the dough to it.

6. Top the dough with the zucchini stem slices and corn, drizzle any remaining garlic-infused oil (and garlic) from the pan on top (you might not need all of the oil), and top with the mozzarella and jalapeño. Bake until the crust is well browned, 8 to 12 minutes.

7. Top with the fresh basil, cut into slices, and serve immediately—the basil will start to brown from the heat.

SWEET CORN AND JALAPEÑO PIZZA WITH ZUCCHINI STEMS

¼ cup extra virgin olive oil

2 or 3 garlic cloves, minced

2 to 5 zucchini stems, very thinly sliced into rounds

Corn kernels cut from 1 ear of corn

8 ounces to 1 pound pizza dough

Cornmeal, for dusting the pizza stone

4 to 6 ounces fresh mozzarella, thinly sliced or torn into small pieces

½ jalapeño or serrano pepper, ribs and seeds removed if you want to reduce the heat, thinly sliced (you might not use all of it—save any extras for Jalapeño Tequila, page 150)

Small handful of fresh basil leaves and/or other fresh herbs, any large leaves torn into pieces

RECIPE INDEX—
Through the Menu

CONVERSION TABLES

Please note that all conversions are approximate but close enough to be useful when converting from one system to another.

OVEN TEMPERATURES

FAHRENHEIT	GAS MARK	CELSIUS
250	½	120
275	1	140
300	2	150
325	3	160
350	4	180
375	5	190
400	6	200
425	7	220
450	8	230
475	9	240
500	10	260

NOTE: Reduce the temperature by 20°C (68°F) for fan-assisted ovens.

APPROXIMATE EQUIVALENTS

1 stick butter = 8 tbs = 4 oz = ½ cup = 115 g

1 cup all-purpose presifted flour = 4.7 oz

1 cup granulated sugar = 8 oz = 220 g

1 cup (firmly packed) brown sugar = 6 oz = 220 g to 230 g

1 cup confectioners' sugar = 4½ oz = 115 g

1 cup honey or syrup = 12 oz

1 cup grated cheese = 4 oz

1 cup dried beans = 6 oz

1 large egg = about 2 oz or about 3 tbs

1 egg yolk = about 1 tbs

1 egg white = about 2 tbs

LIQUID CONVERSIONS

U.S.	IMPERIAL	METRIC
2 tbs	1 fl oz	30 ml
3 tbs	1½ fl oz	45 ml
¼ cup	2 fl oz	60 ml
⅓ cup	2½ fl oz	75 ml
⅓ cup + 1 tbs	3 fl oz	90 ml
⅓ cup + 2 tbs	3½ fl oz	100 ml
½ cup	4 fl oz	125 ml
⅔ cup	5 fl oz	150 ml
¾ cup	6 fl oz	175 ml
¾ cup + 2 tbs	7 fl oz	200 ml
1 cup	8 fl oz	250 ml
1 cup + 2 tbs	9 fl oz	275 ml
1¼ cups	10 fl oz	300 ml
1⅓ cups	11 fl oz	325 ml
1½ cups	12 fl oz	350 ml
1⅔ cups	13 fl oz	375 ml
1¾ cups	14 fl oz	400 ml
1¾ cups + 2 tbs	15 fl oz	450 ml
2 cups (1 pint)	16 fl oz	500 ml
2½ cups	20 fl oz (1 pint)	600 ml
3¾ cups	1½ pints	900 ml
4 cups	1¾ pints	1 liter

WEIGHT CONVERSIONS

U.S./U.K.	METRIC	U.S./U.K.	METRIC
½ oz	15 g	7 oz	200 g
1 oz	30 g	8 oz	250 g
1½ oz	45 g	9 oz	275 g
2 oz	60 g	10 oz	300 g
2½ oz	75 g	11 oz	325 g
3 oz	90 g	12 oz	350 g
3½ oz	100 g	13 oz	375 g
4 oz	125 g	14 oz	400 g
5 oz	150 g	15 oz	450 g
6 oz	175 g	1 lb	500 g

Index

Note: Page references in *italics* indicate photographs.

A

Aebleskivers, potato water and chive, 139–40
Aioli:
  celery leaf, 60
  cheater's, 15–17, *16*
Alcohols, infused (and water), 148–49, *148–49*
Any-season strata, *36*, 36–37
Apple(s):
  cores, freezing, 2
  core syrup, Danish pancakes with, 3–5, *4*
  peel chips, dried, 5
  peels, making tea with, 2
Aquafaba:
  about, 7
  brownies, fudgy, *8*, 9–10
  mayonnaise, 11
  mayonnaise, spicy, 11, *12*
  mayonnaise, spicy, elote with, *12*, 13
  whipping, note about, 7
Artichoke(s):
  leaf nachos with feta and black olives (and cheater's aioli), 15–17, *16*
  using scraps from, 14
Asian ingredients, xviii
Asparagus:
  end, charred, pesto, 21–22
  fibrous parts, trimming, 20
  woody ends, uses for, 20

B

Avocado(s):
  cashew pulp onigirazu, 127–28
  pasta with a crunchy cilantro stem sprinkle, *98, 99*

Bacon ends, buying, 23
Bacon-y tomato jam, 24
Balsamic strawberry jam vinaigrette, 107
Banana(s):
  peel cake with brown sugar frosting, 26–27, *27*
  peels, uses for, 25
  storing, xxi
Basic sautéed beet greens, 29
Basil:
  charred asparagus ends pesto, 21–22
  just-barely-, buttermilk dressing, 97
  –tomato seed dressing, 155
  whipped cream, watermelon rind–lime granita with, 116–18, *117*
Bean cooking liquid. *See* Aquafaba
Bean(s):
  black, and green tomato pico de gallo, 156, *157*
  brothy, with roasted garlic and Parmesan rind, *72, 73*
  kale stem hummus, *109*, 109–10
  lemony olive oil–poached broccoli stems and chickpeas on ricotta toast, *44*, 45

white, and cauliflower core puree with green olive gremolata, 56, *57*
Beer, in Cheddar nub pub cheese, 70
Beet(s):
  greens, basic sautéed, 29
  greens, uses for, 28
  greens and eggplant pizza, 30–31
  greens salad with warm goat cheese rounds, 34–35
  peel margarita, 32, *33*
  peels, uses for, 28
  peel tequila, 150
  roasting directions, 35
Berries:
  washing and storing, xx
  see also specific berries
Bitters, for recipes, xix
Blenders, xxiii
Bloody Mary, dill pickle brine, 133
Blueberry(ies):
  jalapeño margarita, 150
  and lemon, cantaloupe pulp overnight oats with, 119
Blue cheese spread with pecans, 71
Bone-based stocks, preparing, 129–30
Bonito flakes, about, 147
Brandy:
  vanilla pod, 150
  vanilla pod, hot toddy, 164
Breadcrumb(s):
  crispy, fried eggs, *40*, 41
  dried, how to make, 39
  fresh, 39

ACKNOWLEDGMENTS

In the epilogue for *Ratio*, Michael Ruhlman wrote that his impulse to write books originated in the urge to find out what he doesn't know. It was enormously comforting. I've learned a lot both in the making of this cookbook and from the many people who have covered this topic before and continue to break new ground on it now.

Thank you to my editor, Liz Davis—for finding me, advocating for me, and holding my hand through the birth of this book. Thank you to Penny De Los Santos, Nora Singley, Sara Abalan, Lisa Hollander, and Anne Kerman for bringing my recipes to life so beautifully—and to the entire amazing team at Workman.

Thank you to all of the people who helped me get *Cooking from Scraps* from concept to proposal to contract: Kate Bek, Kristen Miglore, Andrea Nguyen, Kenzi Wilbur, Jessica Wicha, and Brittany Zeller-Holland.

Thank you to my gaggle of recipe testers, who made every recipe in this cookbook stronger with their thoughtful feedback: Kate Bek, Corinna Borden, Davy Darnton, Alexa Ellswood, Erin Fisher, Morgan Gilreath, Emily Nichols Grossi, Laura Haggard, Allie and John Healy, Kristi and Emily Healy, Sierra Imwalle, Caroline Lange, Seth Little, Diane "Momma" Pfent, Michelle Rober, Karl Rosaen, Nicole Rossi, Alison Schweiss, and Alison Marie Szymanski.

Thank you to everyone whose name appears in this book; whether you unknowingly inspired a recipe or taught me a neat trick, I am truly grateful.

Thank you to the Food52 team and community, you inspire me every day and I am a better cook because of all of you.

Thank you to my Real Time Farms crew: Cara and Karl Rosaen and Corinna Borden. In large part, I am where I am today thanks to the time spent in a living room with all of you.

Thank you to all of my friends and family near and far who jumped up and down and squealed along with me in excitement, and provided many a pep talk.

Thank you to my husband, Michael, for being a constant source of strength and encouragement. And for, despite being terrible at lying, having the ability to say "this looks delicious!" anytime I set a dish in front of him.

Thank you to my daughter, Josephine, for adamantly refusing to try dishes that "don't look good" and keeping me humble. And for leading a "Mama is the best cooker!" chant when I make something especially beloved—like boxed mac and cheese.

And if you've read down through this entire thing, wondering if your name was going to appear, it likely should have. I apologize for my oversight and thank you wholeheartedly.

Thank you to my tribe of people—I couldn't have done this without your help.

ABOUT THE AUTHOR

Lindsay-Jean Hard received her master's degree in urban planning from the University of Michigan. Her education and passion for sustainability went on to inform and inspire her work in the garden, home, and community. Today she works to build and connect new communities as a food editor and writer. The seeds of this book were planted in her Food52 column of the same name. She lives, writes, loves, and creates in Ann Arbor, Michigan.